PARADISE LOST
Ideal and Tragic Epic

TWAYNE'S MASTERWORK STUDIES
Robert Lecker, General Editor

The Bible: A Literary Study
by John H. Gottcent

The Birth of Tragedy: A Commentary
by David Lenson

The Canterbury Tales: A Literary Pilgrimage
by David Williams

Great Expectations: A Novel of Friendship
by Bert G. Hornback

Heart of Darkness: Search for the Unconscious
by Gary Adelman

The Interpretation of Dreams: Freud's Theories Revisited
by Laurence M. Porter

Jane Eyre: Portrait of a Life
by Maggie Berg

Moby-Dick: Ishmael's Mighty Book
by Kerry McSweeney

The Scarlet Letter: A Reading
by Nina Baym

Sons and Lovers: A Novel of Division and Desire
by Ross C Murfin

To the Lighthouse: The Marriage of Life and Art
by Alice van Buren Kelley

The Waste Land: A Poem of Memory and Desire
by Nancy K. Gish

PARADISE LOST
Ideal and Tragic Epic

FRANCIS C. BLESSINGTON

Twayne Publishers • Boston
A Division of G.K. Hall & Co.

Paradise Lost: Ideal and Tragic Epic
Francis C. Blessington

Twayne's Masterwork Studies No. 12

Copyright 1988 by G.K. Hall & Co.
All rights reserved.
Published by Twayne Publishers
A Division of G.K. Hall & Co.
70 Lincoln Street
Boston, Massachusetts 02111

Typeset in 10/14 Sabon with Trump Mediaeval
display type by Compset, Inc., of Beverly, Massachusetts

Printed on permanent/durable acid-free paper
and bound in the United States of America

Library of Congress Cataloging-in-Publication Data

Blessington, Francis C., 1942–
  Paradise lost.

  (Twayne's masterwork studies ; no. 12)
  Bibliography: p.
  Includes index.
  1. Milton, John, 1608–1674. Paradise lost.
I. Title. II. Series.
PR3562.B534 1988   821'.4   87-21089
ISBN 0-8057-7969-8
ISBN 0-8057-8020-3 (pbk.)

In Memoriam

Professor Raymond E. Blois
(1913–1980)

Contents

.

Preface and Acknowledgments

I intend this study of *Paradise Lost* to be basic and introductory, though I have not hesitated to add new interpretations where I thought them necessary. Ideas are discussed in relation to character and story in order to make Milton more accessible. For beginning students, it may be useful to add that all my attempts at making Milton more understandable are meant to preserve the dignity of the poem, which is unassailable from any quarter, and that no criticism is meant as a substitute for the poem.

I am grateful to Professor Robert Lecker, the series editor, for offering me this chance to write about *Paradise Lost* from many viewpoints. I am grateful also to those candid students who over the years have confessed their difficulties with the poem. Thanks also to Anne Jones of Twayne for her cooperation, to Professor Ann Taylor, my wife, for her scrutiny of the text, to Professor Barbara K. Lewalski for continued professorial assistance, and to the late Professor Raymond E. Blois, who first made Milton real to me.

I gratefully acknowledge the support of Northeastern University's Research and Scholarship Development Fund, which assisted me in the completion of this manuscript.

All references to Milton's poetry are from *John Milton: Complete Poetry and Major Prose*, ed. Merritt Y. Hughes (New York: Odyssey, 1957). *Paradise Lost* is cited parenthetically by book and line. All references to the prose are from *Complete Prose of John Milton*, ed. Don M. Wolfe, et al., 8 vols. (New Haven: Yale University Press, 1953–82), and are cited parenthetically as *Prose*, with volume and page.

Milton as a Cambridge student,
ca. 1629. Artist unknown.
Courtesy of the National Portrait Gallery, London.

Chronology:
John Milton's Life and Works

1608	9 December: John Milton born in Bread St., London, near the Mermaid Tavern, where Shakespeare, Jonson, and their circle gathered. Son of Sara Jeffrey, and John, a composer and a scrivener (moneylender and lawyer). Older sister, Anne.
1615	Brother, Christopher, born.
1616	23 April: death of William Shakespeare.
1619?	Tutored by Thomas Young, highly skilled in languages, especially Latin, who is the subject of Elegy IV.
1620	Becomes a "pigeon" of St. Paul's School, established by the English humanist John Colet. Studies Greek, Latin, Hebrew, French, and Italian; reads Spenser and Du Bartas (in Sylvester's translation). Friendship with Charles Diodati. Graduates in 1624 or 1625.
1621	John Donne becomes Dean of Saint Paul's Cathedral.
1625	Because of fair appearance, nicknamed "The Lady of Christ's" College, Cambridge. Writes academic exercises (*Prolusions*). Quarrels with tutor, William Chappell (cf. *Elegy* I). Writes elegies on Lancelot Andrewes and on other notables.
1629	December: "I am singing the heaven-descended King, the bringer of peace" (52); writes "On the Morning of Christ's Nativity," his first major poem and a serious dedication of self to poetry.
1630	Sonnet "On Shakespeare" for the second edition of the Shakespeare Folio.
1631	Two poems on Hobson the mail carrier and one on the Marchioness of Winchester. (?) "L' Allegro" and "Il Penseroso."
1632	3 July: M.A. cum laude. Retires to Hammersmith for private study, especially of classical literature (also of music and mathematics). Writes first pastoral, *Arcades*.

1634	Writes and has performed *A Mask* (called *Comus* from the eighteenth century on).
1635	Continues retirement at Horton. Incorporated M.A. at Oxford, where he consults books in the Bodleian Library.
1637	Year of crisis. 3 April: death of mother. (6 August: death of Ben Jonson.) 10 August: death of Edward King, the Cambridge companion who inspires *Lycidas*. "Corrected" copy of *Comus* presented to his patron, the Earl of Bridgewater.
1638	Leaves for continent. In Paris meets Dutch jurist and theologian Hugo Grotius. Travels to Nice, then to Genoa, Leghorn, Pisa, and Florence, where he is welcomed by two Italian learned societies, the Svoglati, before whom he reads a Latin poem, and the Apatisti. Continues travels to Siena, Rome, and Naples, where he meets Giovanni Battista Manso, once patron of the Italian epic poet, Torquato Tasso.
1639	Writes *Manso,* showing dedication of self to epic poetry. In England, the First Bishops' War, a conflict over the Church of England's authority in Scotland, breaks out, prelude to the English Civil War. Milton turns toward home. Back in Rome hears rumors of threats against his life by militant papists. Returns to Florence, where he meets Galileo, blind and under house arrest. Visits Lucca, Bologna, Ferrara. In Venice ships home books and music; possibly meets Claudio Monteverdi. Travels to Verona, Milan, and Geneva. Writes *Epitaphium Damonis* after learning of the death of Charles Diodati. Milton arrives in England.
1640	(?) Death of sister, Anne. Sets up school in Aldersgate Street for his sister's children, John and Edward Phillips, eight and nine years old, and about half a dozen other students. Further study as a teacher. Outlines biblical dramas on the Fall, "Adam Unparadised," and a "Paradise Lost." But turns to politics.
1641	In the lists: begins vigorous and at times vulgar and humorous pamphleteering in the parliamentary cause against the king and the bishops. Writes *Of Reformation, Of Prelatical Episcopacy, Animadversions.*
1642	Writes *Reason of Church Government* and *Apology against a Pamphlet.* Marries Mary Powell (age 17). Civil War begins. Domestic and political strife separate new couple after only a few months of marriage.
1643	Mary's departure sparks thoughts on "domestic liberty," which formed *Doctrine and Discipline of Divorce.*

Chronology

1644	Great prose works *Of Education* and, on the freedom of the press, *Areopagitica*. First trouble with eyesight begins, though from childhood plagued with headaches.
1645	Moves to Barbican. Defends his divorce tract with *Colasterion* and *Tetracordon*. Attracted to a Miss Davis. *Poems* published by Humphrey Mosely on 6 October. Reunited with Mary after three-year separation.
1646	29 July: birth of first child, Anne.
1647	13 March: death of father. Moves to High Holborn.
1648	25 October: daughter Mary born. (?) *History of Britain*.
1649	30 January: beheading of Charles I by Parliamentarians. 13 March: Milton made Secretary for the Foreign Tongues by the Council of State under Oliver Cromwell. Becomes the image-breaker of the "martyred king" by writing *The Tenure of Kings and Magistrates, Eikonoclastes, Pro Popolo Anglicano Defensio (A Defense of the English People)*. Left eye now blind; right eye failing.
1651	16 March: son, John, born.
1652	Total blindness. 5 May: death of Mary after giving birth to Deborah (2 May). (?) 16 June: death of infant son John.
1654	Writes great *Defensio Secunda (A Second Defense of the English People)*.
1656	12 November: marries Katherine Woodcock.
1657	19 October: daughter Katherine born.
1658	3 February: weakened by childbirth, wife dies, followed by daughter Katherine, 17 March. (?) Begins *De Doctrina Christiana (Christian Doctrine* [published 1825]). 3 September: death of Cromwell.
1659	*A Treatise of Civil Power. Considerations Touching the Likeliest Means.*
1660	*The Readie and Easie Way to Establish a Commonwealth.* (?) *Paradise Lost* begun. Restoration of Charles II. Milton in hiding. Persecution of the Regicides. Milton arrested and imprisoned. Released. Andrew Marvell speaks in Milton's defense. John Garfield, Royalist: "I shall leave him under the rod of correction, wherewith God hath evidenced His particular judgement by striking him blind."[1] Fined a weighty 150 pounds. Moves to Holborn. Moves to Jewin Street.
1663	24 February: marries Elizabeth Minshull. Strife with daughters.

1665	To escape the plague in London moves to Chalfont St. Giles (Buckinghamshire). Thomas Ellwood, Milton's young Quaker friend, reads *Paradise Lost* in manuscript.
1666	Returns to London. Great Fire of London; Bread Street birthplace destroyed.
1667	*Paradise Lost* published in ten books.
1669	Moves to Artillery Walk near Bunhill Fields.
1671	*Paradise Regained* and *Samson Agonistes* published.
1672	*Artis Logicae* (*Art of Logic*) published.
1673	Expanded *Poems* appears.
1674	Second edition of *Paradise Lost* in twelve books. (?) 8 November: death of Milton.

I

Historical Context

The historical context of *Paradise Lost* comprises the biographical, literary, political, and religious aspects of Milton's life.

During the seventeenth century, writers wrote more directly about themselves than in any previous era: diaries, such as John Evelyn's and Samuel Pepys's; spiritual autobiographies, like John Donne's *Meditations*; even the lyric poems of the metaphysical poets and the cavaliers contain much direct autobiography. In a prose treatise, Milton claims that if he were writing a poem he could speak more directly of himself than in prose: "For although a Poet soaring in the high region of his fancies with his garland and singing robes about him might without apology speak more of himself then I mean to do . . ." (Prose, 1:808). Milton's life, we find, not only influenced his epic, but is also part of it. Milton brought autobiography more directly into his writing than any previous English poet, not merely his personal biography but, those parts that he generalized: his dedication to poetry as a sacred calling, his blindness, his alienation from what he saw as the fallen evil world of the Restoration, and his prophetic insight into truth and the future as outlined through his interpretations of Christian history and doctrine. These passages are found throughout the poem, but most

1

directly in the invocations to books 1, 3, 4, 7, and 9. In each case, the voice is not merely that of John Milton, but that of fallen man, poet, and chosen prophet.

But while prophets are always sure of what they want to say, they must cast about for ways of saying it. In all his writing, Milton believed in mastering completely the conventions of a literary form, conventions gathered from both the theory and the practice of earlier great critics and poets. Milton still followed the impulse given to literature by the Renaissance, that rebirth of Greek and Latin sources which nourished his youth. In a key passage from his *Reason of Church Government*, Milton more than hints at his practice:

> Time servs not now, and perhaps I might seem too profuse to give any certain account of what the mind at home in the spacious circuits of her musing hath liberty to propose to her self, though of highest hope, and hardest attempting, whether the Epick form whereof the two poems of *Homer*, and those other two of *Virgil* and *Tasso* are a diffuse, and the book of *Job* a brief model: or whether the rules of *Aristotle* herein are strictly to be kept, or nature to be follow'd, which in them that know art, and use judgement is no transgression, but an inriching of art. (Prose, 1:812–813)

The reference to Aristotle further alludes to the controversies in Italian Renaissance criticism. This reference combined with the other references to models for a longer epic poem, Homer's *Iliad* and *Odyssey*, Virgil's *Aeneid*, and Tasso's *Jerusalem Delivered*, shows Milton's designed imitation of the greatest predecessors of epic poetry. When he writes his own epic twenty years after writing this passage, we find he incorporates a wide field of influences, ranging from the Bible to Sylvester's translation of Du Bartas's *Divine Weeks*. But the immediate generic context is the epic poem as practiced in ancient Greece and Rome and in Renaissance Italy. Milton's great English predecessor was Edmund Spenser, whose *Faerie Queene* was the greatest English epic to date. Milton thought "our sage and serious" Spenser a better teacher than the medieval scholastic philosophers (Prose, 2:516).

Spenser was a philosophical poet who had brought the conventions of epic poetry from Greece, Rome, and modern Italy to England, an act similar to what Milton himself was contemplating. In 1639, Milton seems to have contemplated an epic on King Arthur, thereby following Spenser's example (*Manso*, 83–84). When he wrote *Paradise Lost*, Milton incorporated his earlier conceptions of biblical dramas, called "Paradise Lost" and "Adam Unparadised," which exist in outline in the Trinity manuscript (1640). While Milton included many devices from Elizabethan drama and crossed the drama and the epic in his poem, its primary genre is the epic, though as Milton himself knew, the epic was dying out as a literary genre by the middle of his century (*PL* 9.44). The epic was considered the highest form of literary art by most Renaissance writers, though some agreed with Aristotle that tragedy was the highest form. Part of the enthusiasm for the epic was due to the emergence of the most powerful of modern political forces, nationalism. Epics suitably expressed public sentiments and values, as well as history.

Milton conceived his epic in an atmosphere of patriotism. Even without his trip to the Continent and his political involvement, Milton would have been aware of the epic as national poem. Milton's early conception of the epic reflects this idea: "That what the greatest and choycest wits of *Athens, Rome,* or modern *Italy,* and those Hebrews of old did for their country, I in my proportion with this over and above of being a Christian, might doe for mine" (Prose, 1:812). Once Milton had decided against an Arthuriad (an epic based on the exploits of King Arthur and his knights) and had chosen instead the central Christian story of the Fall as his subject, his epic became more universal, though still written in English and reflecting in part the failure of the English revolution and his part in it. Men of Milton's strong political ardor do not forget or forgive.

England finds other ways into the poem, too, especially in the many reflections upon revolution and the arguments for and against revolt. War, council scenes, demagogues, and tyranny were part of Milton's world for twenty years before he wrote *Paradise Lost*. For some critics the poem has suggested Milton's own guilt in supporting the execution of the king and the Cromwellian regime. But guilt from what we can tell, is not one of Milton's salient emotions. By the time of the Restoration, Milton himself was disillusioned with Cromwell, though still a political radical and opposed to monarchy. Another difference, which the poet would insist on, is that while the kingdom of heaven is justified by God's superiority over men, no human king can claim such distinction. There can be no doubt, however, that Satan's revolt and the questions of power that result from it were derived from Milton's own political experience. Perhaps even the idea that all will be well was felt by Milton sensing that the "Good Old Cause" had done its work, as indeed it had, for no English king after the revolution had such power as kings before and no one later had to fear torture and death at the hands of the bishops.

Inevitably, I have crossed from politics to religion, since they are usually inseparable in the seventeenth century. And it is religion that is the key to the thinking of Milton and his age. Under that appellation, philosophy, politics, and literature group themselves and take their form. It was God who directed the mind towards truth and who set the divine light of reason in man. It was God who decapitated the king. And it was God who wrote *Paradise Lost,* who was the power behind Milton's muse. Whether we take God as His orthodox religious personage, as the power of nature, or as the true and the right, religion was the form in which the seventeenth century writer, almost always, contemplated reality. In literature, the Golden Age poetry of sixteenth-century England yielded to the divine poetry of the seventeenth century. Donne, Herbert, Crashaw, and Vaughan were all meditative and subjective in a religious sense, and almost all the other poets of the early seventeenth century wrote religious verse. It was a turning inward in order to contemplate the inner self, as Descartes had turned philosophy inward and pointed to the subjective nature of human experience. Milton was too much a part of the outside world to write only prayers and hymns, but his poetry is couched in terms of Old Testament Christianity. Yet Milton belonged to those interpreters of the Bible who did not believe in its literal truth but in its metaphorical approach to it. The Bible is a metaphor of the truth (*Christian Doc-*

trine, Prose, 6:133). In this sense, it is like *Paradise Lost* itself. Like the Hebrew prophets in the Bible, which he read every day, Milton saw himself as a teacher, a teacher of values, who believed that what we read has something to do with who we are and who we can become. He shared the Renaissance Italian humanist belief that great literature can make you a better human being, for the great poet is one: "Teaching over the whole book of sanctity and vertu through all the instances of example with such delight to those especially of soft and delicious temper who will not so much look upon Truth herselfe, unlesse they see her elegantly drest, that whereas the paths of honesty and good life appear now rugged and difficult, though they be indeed easy and pleasant, they would then appeare to all men both easy and pleasant though they were rugged and difficult indeed" (Prose, 1:817–18).

II

Importance of the Work

Today we are skeptical of "great" art. Canons are being challenged. The concept of greatness that Matthew Arnold could be sure of and that William Butler Yeats had to defend is often slighted in all the arts for the more personal and the minimalist. W. H. Auden said that great art was only for "High Holidays of the Spirit,"[2] and Lionel Trilling praised E. M. Forster for choosing "not to be great."[3] Few artists now set out to create grand works, as they did even at the beginning of the twentieth century. Such theory and practice must cause us to rethink what constitutes a "great" work of art and what possible meaning a "great" work can have for us now. Suspicion of rhetorical insincerity, the realization of the relativity of taste, and the greater cultural range of the modern world both geographically and historically have combined to change the concept of great art, but they have not negated it. The writer, composer, or painter who does not attempt a great work still studies the masters, usually with more than a wisp of envy for their era, their patrons, and their audience. Most critics and teachers find that they can respond more fully and creatively to masterworks than to less ambitious works. And the public crowds more than ever to the architectural masterpieces, the galleries, and concert halls in search of the lift provided by the grandeur of the past. One question constantly raised by this situation is, how subjective is the response to a great work of art? Is reputation everything, as with the case of the tired tourist who feels enraptured because he has seen a da Vinci, but who was actually mistakenly looking at a hack work beside it? What do the Parthenon, Michelangelo's paintings in the Sistine Chapel, Bach's B Minor Mass, and *Paradise Lost* provide that lesser works do not? Here we must weed out the subjective response as much as possible and separate, as the drawing teacher says, what we see from what is really there.

All art provides a context which we can share. Through the stimulation of our senses we experience something like life, but in an unreal world: a world of sounds, or sights, or words. I shall isolate five qualities that I think make *Paradise Lost* more valuable than most other poems, but what can be said of this poem can also be extrapolated to other masterpieces. The question is all-important now, since great art is on the defensive. The masterpieces will last, of course, but they must now demonstrate their relevance. Fair enough.

The first quality a great work of literature must have is literary context. By adopting the conventions of its art, it connects to a tradition, hence to an audience. This is not the greatest quality but it is an essential one. *Paradise Lost* defines itself as an epic poem through its narrative structure, its division into books, and its use of conventions, such as the addresses to the muse and the descent from heaven. The characters speak in the long, formal, and declamatory manner of the epic characters in Homer's *Iliad* and *Odyssey* and in Virgil's *Aeneid*. In addition Milton makes allusions to these poems, as Virgil made allusions to Homer and as other epic poets, like Tasso and Spenser, did to those same classical predecessors. Many scenes in Milton are closely modeled upon scenes in Homer and Virgil. Much of the action in *Paradise Lost* is divided into the traditional battle scenes and council scenes of epic poetry. In the invocations, the narrator specifically addresses the question of writing this epic poem and its relation to its predecessors.

But Milton also places the poem within other contexts. His purpose "to justify the ways of God to men" sets the poem within the theological context of theodicy, a vindicating of God's ways to man or, to put it in a more secular way, a proof that man's happiness depends more on himself than on external circumstances. The poem, then, has theological and philosophical treatises as a background, as well as religious poetry (e.g., the literature of creation or Hexemeral literature, such as poems written by Du Bartas and Tasso and others). More important, because *Paradise Lost* retells the story of the first three chapters of Genesis and because Milton deliberately parallels himself with Moses, the reputed author of the first five books of the Bible, *Paradise Lost* is biblical commentary. Or perhaps even something on a par with the Bible itself, since Milton asks, like a prophet, for the same inspiration that filled Moses:

> Sing, Heav'nly Muse, that on the secret top
> Of *Oreb,* or of *Sinai* didst inspire
> That Shepherd, who first taught the chosen Seed,
> In the Beginning how the Heav'ns and Earth
> Rose out of *Chaos.*
> (1.6–10)

Milton's context does not end here, a fact that leads to the second quality for a great work: depth. Masterpieces resonate through other things that we know both in literature and in life. Milton's comprehensive context is part of this resonance. His mastery of the epic conventions, his biblical, theological, and philosophical roots send vibrations through our memories that then reinterpret those works in a kind of counterpoint. We feel the pull of a dialogue. But Milton worked on the largest literary scale of dialogue that we know. As Barbara Lewalski has shown, Milton's poem produces overtones on almost all the literature written before him. A system of verbal allusions and genre patterning make *Paradise Lost* assume and revise not only all previous epics, but also tragedy, divine comedy, georgic, love elegy, hymn, pastoral, prophecy, dialogue, scientific treatise, and many more genres.

This resonance does not cease here. Built into the poem are, as John Hollander and others have heard, verbal echoes from Greek, Latin, Hebrew, Italian, and English poetry. There are discussions of concepts: music, poetry, political liberty, the nature of God, the nature of nature, free will, sex, domestic happiness and domestic hell, human history and divine love, the nature of power and the pretexts of rebellion, the interpretation of dreams, the tragedy and naturalness of death, and the longing for immortality, to name a few. We should note also the use of visual images—in particular, Milton's use of the iconography of the Renaissance. Genre, word, idea, and image make the poem dig deeper into the many contexts of our lives. When a writer presents so many ideas with such intelligence, dignity, and force, we think and feel, even if we disagree with him. The great author wins our trust through his intellectual integrity.

A third quality is originality. In addition to mastering great quantities of ideas, feelings, and conventions, the author must contribute something new. His ideas might be revolutionary or he may just perfect in language what was known before. Milton accomplishes both. As a revolutionary, he blends the often conflicting worlds of the classics and Renaissance Christianity. As a perfecter of language, he elevates the English language to its highest level of formality. Scanning the issues of Miltonic criticism, one can see the power of Milton's originality; no other writer, for example, has provided representations of Satan and God in such controversial terms. Satan's power has moved some critics to see in him a version of Milton himself, the demonic revolutionary and destroyer of kings. Milton might have been struck at the effect of the character on his readers, but would have reproved such readings by saying that God has represented the power of Satan through him. Milton has created Satan so forcefully that many who have read *Paradise Lost* can form no other consistent image of him. Nor can they of "the War in Heaven" or prelapsarian life. The verse in which the poem is written, blank verse or unrhymed iambic pentameter, has proved a model for later writers in that form because of its consistency (i.e., not using triple feet, only duple), its flexibility (blank verse risks monotony), and its modulations of speed and tone. All of these effects have contributed to an original picture of the world of spirits and of perfect man and woman. Milton particularized the spiritual and created its verbal image as no writer had before him.

The fourth quality proceeds from the last: memorability. A great writer's words, images, and story, or at least one of these, should be memorable. "Darkness visible," "precious bane," "in dubious battle," "all hell broke loose," "Pandemonium," and other phrases have contributed to our expression as well as to our store of literary titles. The number and the quality of literary allusions to *Paradise Lost* and literary parodies have also shown the poem's memorability:

> And malt does more than Milton can
> To justify God's ways to man.
> —A. E. Housman[4]

> [Adam and Eve]
> Yet pretermitted not the strait Command,
> Eternal, indispensable, to off-cleanse
> From their white elephantin Teeth the stains
> Left by those tastie Pulps that late they chewd
> At supper. . . .
> —Sir Edward Marsh[5]

This is not a matter of mere reputation, for Milton's stylistic originality is what makes the parody recognizable and clever. Milton has become a context, a grammar, for others to use to focus their ideas, feelings, and words. *Paradise Lost* has become a touchstone, something we should know in order to know other things, a touchstone for elevated verse and serious discussion. It has become synonymous with the grand epic style and treatment. It is altimeter as well as vertiginous experience.

The last quality is that the work act as a stimulus, not only for its own time but beyond it, that its universality and timelessness inspire other generations of readers, critics, or writers. *Paradise Lost* has sparked all three. It is, and always has been, in print in many editions.

Importance of the Work

Every major critic since the poem's publication has interpreted and evaluated the poem, and many a critic has started with, and is best known for his work on, *Paradise Lost*. Although modern poets have been as wary of imitating Milton as they have been of imitating Shakespeare, the poem is a manual of prosody, as well as a touchstone for the sublime. But Milton found no lack of imitators in the eighteenth and nineteenth centuries, who freely interpreted and freely imitated what they found in their Milton: Dryden, Pope, Blake, Wordsworth, Byron, Shelley, Keats, Tennyson, to name only the most important. In order to understand literature, it is necessary to know Milton. Furthermore, *Paradise Lost* has inspired operas, ballets, screenplays, and paintings. The poem still inspires both indirectly and directly:

> Here was the strangest pair
> In the world anywhere,
> Eve in the bells and grass
> Kneeling, and he
> telling his story low . . .
> Singing birds saw them go
> Down the dark path to
> The Blasphemous Tree.
> —Ralph Hodgson[6]

III

Critical Reception

It is a truism concerning most great literary works that the history of their critical reception reveals the history of literary criticism. With *Paradise Lost,* the parallel is more than true. The poem has stood chock-a-block with every major critic and method since its publication. Despite all the commentaries that have illuminated it, the poem has, like all grand works of the imagination, triumphed over them, though also partly because of them. Because criticism applies abstract methods, the particularized subtlety of the poem will always elude its being reduced to any one idea or interpretation; criticism works in two dimensions, the poem, like life, in three. Nevertheless criticism has increased, to a great extent has given us, our awareness of the complex sublimity of *Paradise Lost,* which readers have always felt, from the panegyrics attached to the second edition of the poem in 1674 on. I do not mean that *Paradise Lost* does not have flaws, but that its richness becomes more palpable with every new true critical contribution. We are always learning more of *how* the poem is sublime.

If criticism has enriched *Paradise Lost, Paradise Lost* has rewarded criticism. The Milton criticism of Dryden, Addison, Johnson,

Critical Reception

Blake, Shelley, Hazlitt, Landor, Arnold, Douglas Bush, E. M. W. Till-yard, C. S. Lewis, and many others, including contemporaries, *is* literature, the grand essay inspired by the grand poem. Milton has given critics an elevated subject to praise (or grouse about). The result is sometimes that rare interaction wherein critics find their terms, their enemies, their concepts, their ideologies. The best critics have not painted the poem the color of their own critical thought, like renovators whitewashing frescoed abbey walls, but instead have recorded a discovery inspired by the images and the truths of the poem itself.

On the one hand, we have a species of bardolatry, which is influential because it comes from master writers who uphold Milton's epic as the norm by which to judge other poetic achievements. On the other hand, the more *Paradise Lost* has been examined the more it has not seemed to be heroic poetry in the traditional sense of the term. The praise attached to the second edition of the poem in the verses of Samuel Barrow and Andrew Marvell were echoed by Dryden in his epigram of 1688 in which he elevated Milton to third place in the list of the world's heroic poets. Dryden had met Milton and had turned *Paradise Lost* into a closet opera:

> Three *Poets*, in three distant *Ages* born,
> *Greece, Italy,* and *England* did adorn.
> The *First* in loftiness of thought Surpass'd;
> The *Next* in *Majesty*; in both the *Last*:
> The force of *Nature* could no farther goe:
> To make a *Third*, she joynd the former two.[7]

This poem adorned Tonson's folio edition of 1688. Whether poets praise more in their dedicatory poems than elsewhere, or whether they change their minds in the cooler element of prose, Dryden records a different view of Milton in his "Dedication" to his translation of the *Aeneid* in 1697. There he claims that the three greatest heroic poets are Homer, Virgil, and Tasso. Milton would have been included, if the dragon had not got the girl: "if the Devil had not been his hero, instead of Adam; if the giant had not foiled the knight, and driven him out of his stronghold, to wander through the world with his lady errant; and if there had not been more machining persons than human in his poem."[8] Dryden forecasts the history of Milton criticism: critics have either assumed that Milton's poem is now the standard, or they have recorded their irritation that something is askew in this epic, something unignorable. Milton had tried to write the Christian epic, the story of Eden, but that epic has no hero, unless He is divine, and that kind of hero is not what the human reader usually expects. We must either accept a different definition of heroism or say that heroism as we know it has ended. Milton reconciled Christianity and classical heroism, but the hero has succeeded to loss, endurance, and suffering, however mitigated by prophecy. It is noteworthy that Dryden's metaphors derive from the very conventions of romance that Milton jettisons at the beginning of the climactic book 9. What is important in Dryden's remarks is that the first professional critic in English literature has recorded his frustration at not finding traditional heroic action in Milton's poem. At this crossroads, all other critics will choose between Milton's independence of thought, style, and action or his reliance upon tradition. What all critics will agree upon is that Milton's power has attracted their attention, and sometimes made their careers.

Early commentators contented themselves with drawing classical parallels and with examining Milton as a competitor of Homer and Virgil. The most influential of these critics was Joseph Addison. Using the poetic categories laid down by Aristotle and employed by such French critics as Le Bossu, Addison analyzed the poem in detail, dedicating eighteen *Spectator* papers (1712) to Milton's epic and later collecting them into a book (1719). Addison forced onto the neoclassical literary consciousness the idea that *Paradise Lost* was the greatest epic in any language. But Addison did not just star purple passages; he also found faults and showed how Milton's poem works. His criticism has been unjustly neglected and unjustly criticized for lack of originality. In fact, Addison anticipated much later criticism that he made redundant. Addison's eloquence helped speed Milton's reputation, but it was his attention to detail that showed the rhetorical function of many of

Milton's subtleties: that by beginning in medias res (in the midst of things) Milton achieved plot unity; that the rival kingdom of Hell parallels Virgil's rival kingdom of Carthage; how Milton is influenced by, but improves upon, his sources and makes them his own; that Adam hints to Eve to withdraw during the talk with Raphael so he may discuss her perfections; that Milton modified the tragedy by humiliating Satan and by prophesying the Redemption. Faults Addison deduced from his rigid neoclassical sense of decorum: that allegorical characters are improbable in an epic, that narrators should not intrude upon the action, that Milton's style is sometimes too stiff and over-redolent of learning. In short, he analyzes the poem from its plot to its elisions in the manner of much contemporary criticism. Many of the issues he raises have remained issues: that the divine characters and book 12 are duller than the rest of the poem, that Satan is terrifying and absurd, that Adam and Eve take their conceptions from their natural surroundings, that the landscape of Eden is symbolic, that Milton was thinking of reader response ("he knew all the Arts of Affecting the Mind")[9]. Who could disagree with his method: "A true Critick ought to dwell rather upon Excellencies than Imperfections, to discover the concealed Beauties of a Writer, and communicate to the World such things as are worth their Observation"?[10] Modern commentaries on the poem have drawn heavily on Addison.

Milton elevated and sharpened not only the critical mind but the artistic mind as well. Though Shakespeare exerted an influence through the body of his work, he had no worthy imitators; Milton through the less diffuse influence of one major poem helped many later poets to create. By the eighteenth century Milton had emerged, if not the greatest English poet, at least the greatest English writer in the greatest literary form, epic. By 1720, Dryden's triad of Homer, Virgil, and Milton is so well established that Pope recommends in his preface to his translation of the *Iliad* that every translator of Homer should work with Virgil and Milton open before him. When Pope created his mock-epic *The Rape of the Lock* (1712), he could rely upon his audience to recognize allusions to *Paradise Lost*.

If Pope's influence confirms general opinion, the next major critic transforms our image of the poet. Samuel Johnson drew heavily upon Addison, but his influence has far exceeded that of his source. His *Life of Milton* (1779) has become the most authoritative voice on the poem, the starting place for most critical discussion. Because of Johnson's reputation as character, critic, inventor of literary biography, moralist, and master of letters, even his prejudices have weight. His picture of Milton the man was the result of his royalist intolerance of Milton's Whiggery. It was for later writers to connect the picture Johnson gave with Milton's Satan, but Johnson's intolerance laid the groundwork: "Milton's republicanism was, I am afraid, founded in an envious hatred of greatness, and a sullen desire of independence; in petulance impatient of controul, and pride disdainful of superiority."[11] For Johnson it was immoral of Milton to work for Cromwell, murderer of a king. No mention is made of Milton's many companions. From Johnson, too, comes the unfounded picture of Milton's "Turkish contempt of females as subordinate and inferior beings."[12] The force of Johnson's wit often makes his opinions seem more right than they are.

But unlike some later critics, Johnson separates man and poet. The praise of *Paradise Lost* is unparalleled in Johnson's critical writings: "his work is not the greatest of heroick poems, only because it is not the first."[13] If Addison saw morals buried in the poem, Johnson saw them on the surface, the way each critic preferred them. Johnson proceeds, like Addison, by considering Aristotelian divisions and by listing virtues and flaws, though without Addison's attention to the text. Johnson formulates the aphorisms that shall influence later criticism: "the want of human interest is always felt";[14] "none ever wished it longer than it is."[15] Besides testifying to the difficulty of the poem, Johnson points to other faults: he agrees with Addison that the allegorical figures are improbable because they do more than their symbolic nature allows; that the invocations are out of place in an epic; that the style is artificial and foreign to the English idiom; that puns are one of Milton's weaknesses; that book 6 is written for children. Johnson is the ultra-rationalist; what did Satan do with his spear and shield when he became a toad at the ear of Eve? But he differs from

Critical Reception

Addison in his palliating of almost every fault he accuses the poet of.
Honesty gets the better of prejudice so Johnson can break through the
stranglehold of neoclassical decorum with the admission that "criticism sinks in admiration."[16] Milton has won. The critic must admit
that his conception of poetry is too narrow and unimaginative for the
poem. Such insight and honesty make Johnson the greatest English
critic.

In the romantic era, Milton rose to the status of a demiurge who
influenced every romantic poet. Pope's ironic use of *Paradise Lost* in
his mock-epic appears timid beside romantic transformations. The romantic poets saw Milton as their most direct poetic influence, a force
to be harnessed for their own purposes. Most extreme, and yet typical,
is William Blake, but similar if more restricted use can be found in
Wordsworth, Coleridge, Byron, Keats, and Shelley. Blake thought Milton the greatest English poet. He etched illustrations for *Paradise Lost*
and other poems of Milton. In *Jerusalem* (1804–20), he elevates Milton above Shakespeare and Chaucer. But Milton's belief in reason, the
value of the classics, and other forms of religious and cultural ortho-
doxy disgusted Blake. So Blake found Satan the hero of *Paradise Lost,*
not because he wins, as Dryden thought, but just because: "Note: The
reason Milton wrote in fetters when he wrote of Angels & God, and
at liberty when of Devils & Hell, is because he was a true Poet and of
the Devil's party without knowing it."[17] Blake believed he knew Milton's mind because Milton had appeared to him many times in visions.
Blake's antipathy to authority, reason, the classics, and his own historical moment produced an inverse Milton, whose true hero is Satan,
the representation of the free desire that Milton suppressed in order to
be orthodox. This desire is also represented by Milton's wives and
daughters. Blake's Milton finds himself as Satan one hundred years
after his death, while Blake relegates Milton's God to reason and the
authoritarian testing of mankind. Milton is central to Blake's symbolism. Blake's use of Milton is too complex for this superficial analysis,
but Blake's need to use Milton to establish his own ideas—as in his
epic called *Milton* (1804–8)—begins a tradition of treating *Paradise
Lost* as if the poet's or the critic's mind is its own place and can make

a heaven of hell, a hell of heaven. Because some of Milton's ideas are not popular with later ages and because Milton is too strong a force in literature, he is assumed to have been unconsciously what some later creative minds want him to be. All want Milton in their camp, even as an enemy. Milton now becomes the language for defining one's literary stance. If he arrives at Blake's cottage at Felpham, he turns up also at Oxford, New Haven, and the two Cambridges.

Milton has become the romantic Satanist, who created Satan, or the classical Protestant, who upholds tradition and the grand style. In short, Milton has become the two parts of the modern mind: Satan and God, subjective and objective. The rejecters of the orthodox Milton would probably agree with Blake: "We do not want either Greek or Roman Models if we are but just & true to our Imaginations, those Worlds of Eternity in which we shall live forever in Jesus our Lord."[18] The orthodox stance is stated by William Hazlitt in 1818: "He relied on the justice of his cause, and did not scruple to give the devil his due. Some persons may think that he has carried his liberality too far, and injured the cause he professed to espouse by making him the chief person in his poem. Considering the nature of his subject, he would be equally in danger of running into this fault, from his faith in religion, and his love of rebellion; and perhaps each of these motives had its full share in determining the choice of his subject."[19]

Criticism has now defined two sides: the orthodox, basing itself on what Milton said he said and the subjective, probing what Milton "really did." Those critics following the subjective methods opened up by Blake will have their major interest in what they find between the lines of text; they will psychologize beneath the surface. The orthodox critics will illuminate the text by citing it as evidence. Most critics will be members of the orthodox school from this point on, refining the ways Milton's poem works upon the reader. Their defect, when they have one, will be dullness. The subjective critics will be a vociferous minority who run the risk of falling into subjectivity themselves. Both will be influential, and both will represent the turn thought has taken in literary criticism and elsewhere into objective and subjective experience. Of course, I am oversimplifying: both sides will admit some part of the opposite element, but nonetheless *Paradise Lost* will be the challenge providing subtlety for one school and creativity for the other.

During the nineteenth century, *Paradise Lost* was, as Arnold and Emerson agreed, the sublime English poem. David Masson composed his monumental life of Milton and his times (1859–92). Scholars turned to the poem once English literature was admitted to the curriculum. The earlier emphasis upon classics also promoted interest, since classicists found Milton so congenial he was often cited as a parallel in the notes to classical texts. Walter Alexander Raleigh's study appeared in 1900, analyzing a style, "the most distinguished in our poetry."[20] By this time, the devoted American Miltonist, James Holly Hanford, was reading Milton for the first time. In France, Denis Saurat (1925) controversially analyzed Milton's thought and in England E. M. W. Tillyard (1930) emphasized the changing states of mind in which Milton composed his epic, opening up later reader-response criticism: "The meaning of a poem is not the story told, the statements made, the philosophy stated, . . . and the only way to arrive at this meaning is to examine our minds as we read."[21] Tillyard found Milton's unconscious and conscious meanings in the poem, Milton's Satanic "heroic energy" (235), and his rational interior paradise. Tillyard tried to bridge in an orthodox manner the two readings of *Paradise Lost*.

But a reaction had already set in against the poem. T. S. Eliot, Ezra Pound, J. Middleton Murry, F. R. Leavis, and some other modernists agreed that Milton was the poet of sublimity but charged that sublimity had nothing to do with the English tradition. Addison thought that the language was not up to Milton's demands on it. To the Leavisites of the "Cambridge Attack," who followed Eliot, Milton forced the language into a Greco-Roman idiom that broke the tradition of the native style that led from Shakespeare and Donne to Dryden. In 1936, Eliot's ideas were central: "Milton is unsatisfactory. . . . in respect of the deterioration . . . to which he subjected the language."[22] Eliot charged Milton with rhetoric and castigated him for severing poetry from speech, for dissociating thought from feeling. He claimed

Milton's influence was baneful upon later writers and still had to be fought off by contemporary poets. Milton's blindness to sensual experience was the central problem: "Milton may be said never to have seen anything" (162). In 1947, Eliot's second essay on Milton recants somewhat: he praises the uniqueness of Milton's style and the appropriateness of his generalized imagery to the spiritual world he was describing. He also allows Milton as a model for contemporary poets for avoiding colloquial speech and for true freedom in versification. But Eliot's earlier attack continued to reverberate.

Its immediate effect was to shock the complacent professor into defending Milton by defining in just what Milton's greatness consists. Like Milton himself, Milton criticism thrives on controversy. An influential Christian reading of the poem by Charles Williams (1940), C. S. Lewis's *A Preface to Paradise Lost* (1942), and Douglas Bush's *Paradise Lost in our Time* (1945) are permanent contributions to our understanding of *Paradise Lost*. Lewis oriented the poem toward the epic tradition and toward Milton's own theology. Bush saw *Paradise Lost* depicting Milton's vision of the world: his epic and theology were a representation of the universal plight of man everywhere, a depiction of the struggle between good and evil for the soul of man. For Bush, the poem expressed Milton's concern for improving oneself. The poem was an example of "Christian humanism." Part of the criticism that followed in the next two decades was colored by miltonoclasts and miltonolaters.

Most pervasive was the rise of professional criticism in the universities. The proliferation of Milton criticism was outstanding even in an age of critical proliferation. More and more detailed studies appeared within such categories such as source study, style, rhetoric, Satan, and Milton's God. Every theory has been brought to bear: Freudian, reader-response, deconstruction, archetypal, generic tension within the poem (e.g., epic versus drama), the visual arts, music, science, politics, theology, typology. I only allude to these studies here, not because they are of little value, but for the opposite reason. Their plenitude adds immeasurably to our knowledge and enjoyment of the poem. Few Milton studies are valueless, because Milton's breadth has already anticipated a wide range of literary thought and emotion and because *Paradise Lost* attracts, trains, and produces much solid criticism. Today over one hundred and fifty articles and books on Milton appear every year, most of them dealing with *Paradise Lost*. A few break new ground; most refine earlier work. If the bibliography in this book pays scant homage to the work that has been done, the continued growth of Milton criticism shows that every age, perhaps every reader, wishes to create a "reading" of the poem. And always will. Milton criticism has taught us how to read other poems besides *Paradise Lost* and has created part of our system of literary quality. Nothing is wasted; the good criticism is absorbed into the culture, as religion into manners. But after a critical idea has exhausted controversy and emulation, the poem stands, like Samson, a little more in the sun, bold and eager for the next challenger.

A READING

IV

The Story of All Things

The story of *Paradise Lost* is an expansion of the first three chapters of the Book of Genesis in the Bible, the story of the creation of the earth and man and of man's fall. To the account of creation and the fall, Milton added summaries of biblical history and, most important, the fall of Satan, which Milton gathered from many sources, since there is no standard account. This background does not imply Milton's lack of creativity but the opposite: Milton risked telling the story every reader knew. His task was to deepen, expand, and add dramatic detail to it. First, he did not tell the story in the biblical sequence of events, but employed flashbacks and flashforwards, in an effort to make a statement about time itself. Second, Milton imagined for himself what no one knew or could know: what the ideal life of heavenly beings is and what supernatural man and woman would be like. For this purpose, he ransacked almost every major work of literature, especially Greek, Roman, and Italian works, as well as works of art, music, science, philosophy, and theology. But Milton could absorb these works and still maintain his own independent style and thought. He is never mechanical in his use of his sources. As a result, his work is at the same time encyclopedic and personal. His talent was always to imagine his poetry completely, to find room in Eden, heaven, and hell for his own exalted vision of freedom and love.

The chronology of events in the order they occur in Christian history are simply:

I. The War in Heaven
II. The Creation of Our Universe
III. Adam and Eve in Paradise
IV. The Temptation and Fall of Man
V. The Aftermath of the Fall: Human History.

Milton, following the tradition of epic poetry, changes the order of the action in his plot (the numerals here refer to books):

I.–II. Poem begins after Satan's army is defeated. Council in hell.
III. Council in Heaven. The Father and Son react to Satan's resolution to take revenge on man. Son offers His life for man.
IV. Adam and Eve in Eden, including a flashback to Eve's creation.
V.–VI. The Angel Raphael tells Adam the story of the War in Heaven (flashback).
VII. Raphael tells the story of the creation of the universe (flashback).
VIII. Adam recounts his creation (flashback).
IX. Temptation and Fall.
X. Aftermath of the Fall on Earth and in Hell.
XI.–XII. Michael reveals to Adam the future course of biblical history (flashforward).

The plot is comprehensive: it tells the story of life from its beginning to its end within the framework of Christian history, but it is not limited by that history. Because of its techniques of prophesying the future and of distilling even Christianity itself to an essential myth, the poem goes beyond religion. Its symbolism and allegory transcend Milton's religious and historical moment. We must read *Paradise Lost* the way Milton read the Bible: symbolically. The plot is a metaphor for human experience: its drives to power, its need for love and forgiveness, its relationships between the sexes, its need for society, its yearning to live forever, its. . . . There is no way to limit the plot of the poem. As Samuel Barrow said in his Latin poem attached to the 1674 edition of *Paradise Lost*: "He who reads *Paradise Lost* what does he read but everything? All things and the origins of all things" (1–3; my translation).

V

Hell: Darkness Visible

SATAN

The power of Milton's Satan has been acknowledged by all readers of the poem. To the Satanist school, he represents Milton's own inner nature, repressed by the Christian era he was devoted to. To the orthodox critics, Satan is the traditional power of evil, a creature destroyed by his own ambition. Both schools are right. If Milton had not been able to feel and imagine the power of rebelliousness, he would have denied his own biography. The breaker of king and bishops had to know the thrill of rebellion. But Milton also acknowledged consciously the need to repress such power when in the service of wrongdoing. That Milton had almost as much Satan, or perhaps more, as God in him allowed him to create the most disturbing and powerful rendition of the archetypal villain. Milton's Satan has colored even our reading of the Bible, where Satan receives no such consistent and direct treatment. What the New Testament only alludes to, Milton dramatizes: Satan as the pure will to power regardless of the means. One can say, of course, that because Milton's devil is so powerful compared to his God, Milton was of the devil's party without knowing it; but the comment remains, for lack of other evidence (Milton was never psychoanalyzed), subjective. All we can do is admit the unforgettable strength of Milton's Satan, his nobility in suffering for his cause, and his base destruction of weaker creatures to achieve his ends. Satan's story is that of cosmic frustration. In the conscious context of *Paradise Lost*, he is unconditionally corrupt.

Perhaps we can get a better understanding of Satan by examining his roots. Villains in literature seldom receive their due; classical villains, for example, are grotesques and never possess the qualities of heroes. The nobility Aristotle required of an epic hero would exclude Satan from the epic, and classical drama had little use for total villains. Elizabethan drama featured the machiavel, and Milton made good use of the Fausts and Iagos he found there. But these villains were not given full epic treatment. Tasso's antagonists, though epic, are much less effective than Satan. No other examples need to be considered. (Epigones, like Byronic heroes and Captain Ahab, owe some of their power to Milton.) Milton then crossed the archetypal villain of Christianity—only absolute religions like this can produce complete villains at all—with the Vice from the Elizabethan stage. Milton's treatment was not allegorical. He dramatized the Vice and set him center stage, unlike a medieval devil or a Comus who runs at the coming of powerful virtue. Satan's power is awesome. Evil in other great poems is more under control—we can relax with goodness. But not in *Paradise Lost*. God's permissive will allows Satan full reign, as He does in the Book of Job. The human race is in Satan's power: he is the author of death and all suffering. God laughs at Satan's actions but we can't—assuming we sympathize at least vicariously with Milton's Christian readership. We can only turn to God who lets Satan have this life: rewards and punishments are to come. We must agree with Adam: "Subtle he needs must be, who could seduce / Angels" (9.307–8).Through Adam and Eve, we feel Satan's destructiveness. Through Satan, we feel human life's insecurity, a risk few artists have been willing to take. The result is terrifying.

But the result of Satan's action is his own damnation, too. So, in a sense, he is tragic. Few would dispute that Satan produces the fear required of tragedy, but does he produce the pity? Modern readers who are beyond the scope of traditional Christianity do not have the same reactions to Satan as the seventeenth-century reader did. Most modern readers do not feel that Satan is the instigator of all our woe. After a century and a half of antiheroes, we might not automatically assume that Satan is a villain at all, though we must keep in mind that Milton's audience did. But do we feel pity for Satan? If so, he could qualify as a tragic hero. Satan's fight against the hierarchy of heaven has the potential for a romantic tragedy: the proponent of freedom fighting the establishment of an omnipotent God. But Milton is not Shelley. Absolute rule in heaven is a given for Milton, though he would allow no such rule on earth. Yet there is so much identification, or "negative capability," in his portrait that Milton presents Satan sympathetically at certain points. Satan is struck by the beauty of Paradise and by the love of Adam and Eve. The sorrow revealed in his soliloquy to the sun depicts him as a victim of his own nature, an urge to power that is in conflict with the world it lives in and even Satan wishes it away in a Faustian mood:

> Which way I fly is Hell; myself am Hell;
> . . . . .
> O then at last relent: is there no place
> Left for Repentance, none for Pardon left?
> None left but by submission; and that word
> *Disdain* forbids me, and my dread of shame
> Among the Spirits beneath, whom I seduc'd.
> (4.75, 79–83)

But such moments are rare. Satan admits that in spite of "*disdain*," he had "the same free Will and Power to stand" (4.66). But by *disdain* Satan means that submission to God's will is beneath his dignity. *Disdain* derives from the Latin *disdignari,* to think unworthy, to treat with scorn. Satan's objection is that he can never be anything other than ruler himself; to submit to God is not to be thought of. Satan is the embodiment of the principle of self-will and for that reason is antisocial. What makes Satan more attractive to the modern reader is the antipathy many modern readers feel for the "authoritarian" government of heaven. We may feel a moment's sympathy for Shakespeare's Richard III when he loses his horse in battle and then his life, but no one feels that he did not deserve his fate. But in *Paradise Lost,* the conqueror has, unlike Henry Tudor, an omnipotence and a control of events that is never shaken. Few thinking readers can accept such authoritarianism even in a divine being. But Milton accepted and employed this now unpopular Christian concept. Every great work of literature partakes somewhat of the age that produced it. In order to see Satan as he logically functions in Milton's epic, we must think partly in seventeenth-century terms. Seen in this way, Satan's villainy overrides our sympathies.

But if Satan does not receive our pity, he must receive our admiration. He represents power without morality. Our difficulty in evaluating Satan and our admiration for his character are evident in the spate of criticism on *Paradise Lost.* Milton gives the devil his due but balances Satan's force with the power of the Father and with the authority of the narrator; Satan's speeches try to convince us that he is great and good, while heaven and the narrator try to convince us of the opposite. In the beginning of the poem, Satan stands center stage. He speaks to his followers in order to convince them that action, even revenge, is better than the acceptance of defeat. While the seventeenth-century reader would assume that Satan is lying, since he always postures, few readers of any period can be insensitive to the power of his words and hence to the power of evil:

> Farewell happy Fields
> Where Joy for ever dwells: Hail horrors, hail
> Infernal world, and thou profoundest Hell
> Receive thy new Possessor: One who brings
> A mind not to be chang'd by Place or Time.
> The mind is its own place, and in itself
> Can make a Heav'n of Hell, a Hell of Heav'n.
> (1.249–55)

No audience could miss the epic tone and the sound of great poetry; Milton's verse itself confesses that evil is powerful. Even if the narrator has claimed that Satan's speeches reveal the fallen archangel to be "Vaunting aloud, but rackt with deep despair" (1.126), his grandeur overrides this authorial commentary. We feel Satan is heroic as a survivor, as a rebel, as a defier of defeat. But Satan's grandness is ruined by his destructiveness: "To do aught good never will be our task, / But ever to do ill our sole delight" (1.159–60). Milton asks us to measure Satan by the yardstick of morality, not by attitude or achievement. He forces us to admit that powerful qualities are useless if destructive. The real parallel to Satan is Hitler; both embody power insensitive to means. So he confesses: "my dread of shame / Among the Spirits beneath, whom I seduc'd / With other promises and other vaunts" (4.82–84). Always Satan has qualities—here honesty—but we must in the context of the poem measure means by ends: Satan is plotting our death.

We may, of course, take other approaches to the poem. I have stayed so far on the level of Milton's conscious and Christian meaning. We may speculate on what Satan means psychologically and biographically, especially if we feel that Milton's God does not have the force of his devil. Here we run the risk of being subjective, but we must remember that Blake and Shelley felt this as well as other readers. Is there an artistic failure on Milton's part of not balancing his forces well and thereby losing control of his meaning? One way around this assumption, as we shall see, is to analyze how much of Satan's power derives from his own words: it is Satan after all, who tells us that he shook the throne of heaven with his legions and that the battle was doubtful in its outcome. It is not until the flashback to the battle itself that we discover Satan bested by the lesser angel, Abdiel, Satan not even striking a blow. The action of the poem gradually unmasks Satan's rhetoric. When we see Satan in action, often he is lying, misleading, working by innuendo. He lies about the Son's vice-regency, saying that the Son is taking over heaven. He lies to Eve in the form of a serpent, saying he has gained the faculty of speech from eating of the forbidden fruit. He rarely confronts his divine enemy directly and settles for revenge against the weaker Adam and Eve, an action unworthy of a classical or epic hero. Satan does not lose all his noble qualities, but those very qualities make him and the human race unhappy. Finally we must choose between an exciting rebel and a destructive maniac. Satan has more power than any villain in history, but also more evil. His qualities—willfulness, courage, endurance—dwindle in the long run to anger, envy, and despair. Milton was always concerned about the long run.

Milton's moral emphasis hinges upon the free will of his characters. Whatever we think about the determinacy of human action, Milton's poem presents characters who act freely. Even Satan, who insists that disdain forbids him to repent, admits that he chose his course freely (4.66-72). The paradox, if there is one, is Milton's belief that inclination can be held in check by will. Moreover, we see characters act freely and claim to act freely. Milton's characters soliloquize frequently and through their soliloquies we learn that they are aware of their own choices and actions. Even when characters fall, they do so knowing their failures.

We can see almost all of Satan's virtues and defects in his approach to Eden. After Satan leaves hell, the reader gradually gains a heavenly perspective on Satan. In hell we had only the narrator's comments to assure us that Satan was glozing over despair with rhetoric. In Eden, Uriel sees through the mask, but not before Satan has passed by pretending to be a cherub; when Satan alights on earth, Uriel notices Satan's "ire, envy and despair" (4.115). Once in Eden, Satan reveals the noble characteristics that he still possesses. First, wonder at spotting Adam and Eve:

> O Hell! what do mine eyes with grief behold,
> Into our room of bliss thus high advanc't
> Creatures of other mould, earth-born perhaps,
> Not spirits, yet to heav'nly Spirits bright
> Little inferior; whom my thoughts pursue
> With wonder, and could love, so lively shines
> In them Divine resemblance, and such grace
> The hand that form'd them on thir shape hath pour'd.
> (4.358-65)

If admiration leads Satan to the brink of love, his commitment to revenge leads him to sympathy:

> Ah gentle pair, yee little think how nigh
> Your change approaches, when all these delights

Will vanish and deliver ye to woe,
More woe, the more your taste is now of joy.
(4.366–69)

Inaudibly, he tells Adam and Eve that God is to blame for wronging Satan, not Satan for wronging them, which is only a consequence of God's actions. Satan ends by confessing his crime before he commits it. His premeditation belies any act of passion:

And should I at your harmless innocence
Melt, as I do, yet public reason just,
Honor and Empire with revenge enlarg'd,
By conquering this new World, compels me now
To do what else though damn'd I should abhor.
(4.388–92)

Satan's whole character is revealed here in miniature: his partly admirable nature, his intelligence, his awareness, his cunning, his powers of speech, his determination, and his monomania. Satan's own nature is further ruined as he plans to ruin Adam and Eve's: all his talents are in the service of his thwarted passion for power. If he cannot be vice-regent in heaven, there shall be nothing else, if he can destroy it. We may admire Satan as a hero only if we deny his social and political aspects, only if we cut him out of his context and view him as part of ourselves, as a dramatization of our id. But *Paradise Lost* is a public poem, illustrating the effects of egoism on history at large. To compare great things to small, Satan is a social disease.

Much of Satan's power stems from rhetoric. Early in the poem his heroic stance is created merely by what he says. At first Satan boasts that "The mind is its own place, and in itself / Can make a Heav'n of Hell, a Hell of Heav'n" (1.254–55). Yet Satan immediately lures the rebel angels to seek revenge on earth. Milton could have opened the poem with Satan in the last stages of battle, but the structure as is allows Satan to create a heroic world out of words:

Innumerable force of Spirits arm'd
That durst dislike his reign and mee preferring,

Hell

> His utmost power with adverse power oppos'd
> In dubious Battle on the Plains of Heav'n,
> And shook his throne.
> (1.101–05)

He maintains this fiction even to Gabriel and the guards of Eden:

> Not that I less endure, or shrink from pain,
> Insulting Angel, well thou know'st I stood
> Thy fiercest, when in Battle to thy aid
> The blasting volley'd Thunder made all speed
> and seconded thy else not dreaded Spear.
> (4.925–29)

It is not till book 6 that we see Satan easily bested by Abdiel and Michael, not Gabriel, and discover that he never landed a blow. Just as Satan returns to his own shape with the touch of Ithuriel's spear when the Adversary is disguised as a toad at the ear of Eve, truth removes Satan's disguises.

Gabriel further unmasks Satan by revealing that he was hypocritical, even in heaven:

> And thou sly hypocrite, who now wouldst seem
> Patron of liberty, who more than thou
> Once fawn'd, and cring'd, and servily ador'd
> Heav'n's awful Monarch? wherefore but in hope
> To dispossess him, and thyself to reign?
> (4.957–61)

Satan's manner is more Iago's than Othello's. His tragedy is the "romantic" one of rebelling against society, but not out of principle, out of disappointment at being second to any authority. In another poem we might side with such a character, and there are those readers who do side with Satan, but the poem as a whole works against this interpretation. In order to heroize Satan, we must feel that the authority he revolts against deserves it.

We do not experience the revolt in heaven until the middle of the poem. By then Satan's heroic posture is unravelling with the tapestry

35

that he has woven with words. It is words that seduce men and angels in *Paradise Lost,* and elsewhere. Satan lies to the angels of the north and to Eve. His many disguises—cherub, cormorant, tiger, serpent, mist—reveal his chameleon nature. He can become anything, except a loyal subject. While events up till the middle of the poem show Satan strong in defiance, we see little of his heroism, except for his bold taunting of Gabriel and the other guardians of Eden. The justice of Satan's cause lies in his claims concerning the Son's tyranny. Here Milton had no sources he had to rely upon, though the notion that Satan revolted against the exaltation of the Son was current at the beginning of the seventeenth century.

In order to understand the religious issues of *Paradise Lost,* we must divest ourselves of our preconceptions concerning Christianity. Like a great religious painting by Raphael, for instance, the images provide all we need to know about the action. Milton would have insisted on doctrinal aspects of his epic, "exemplary to a Nation" (Prose, 1:815), but, unlike much purely religious verse, such as Du Bartas's *Divine Weeks,* Milton's epic is still read today, for it has a poetic life of its own, a life beyond its Christian message. Milton provides us with the evidence to judge Satan ourselves. In book 5, the Father proclaims the Son vice-regent of heaven. We feel his choice is justified because the Son helped create Satan and the rebel angels as well as our world. Earlier in the poem, though later in time, the Son's offer of self-sacrifice for man on the cross further justifies the choice.

Satan reacts in the pattern established in book 1: he stirs Beelzebub to help him gather the angels of the north for a council in which he lies and insinuates, so they follow his predetermined course of action. Satan tells Beelzebub that the Son will come like an emperor in triumph and give new laws. He further insinuates that to utter more is not safe, as if thought police are afoot. The creation of such tension is a standard subversive ploy. Satan's real impulses are demonstrated imagistically when he appears for the debate perched upon the same mount on which the Son was proclaimed vice-regent. It is up to Satan now to show that he merits the vice-regency.

Instead, Satan reveals that he has always resented the Father's power: "too much to one, but double how endur'd" (5.783). Satan claims to have been "self-begot" (5.860), punning upon the Father's elevation of the Son whom "This day I have begot" [i.e., made king] (5.603) and contradicting his own statement earlier in the poem in his soliloquy, "he deserv'd no such return / From me, whom he created what I was" (4.42–43). The split between the bold rhetorical or political Satan and the inner despairing archangel deepens as we move through the poem. Of course, Satan must think he is wronged, just as most criminals feel they are wronged (some are). It is the only way to live morally with one's evil deeds. Moreover Satan does not justify his position, but relies upon preying upon fears of domination among the angels of the north. In book 2, he reflectively lists four reasons to justify his rebellion: "just right," "the fixt Laws of heav'n," "free choice" of him over the Messiah as leader, and "merit" achieved in battle and council (2.18–21). The first, "just right," Satan can hardly claim; the Son's humility, obedience, discipline, and altruistic love that Milton—and Christ—thought essential to exaltation have no place in Satan's insecure nature. The Laws of Heaven may have raised Satan to a place of eminence in the north, but they give him no precedence over the Son, nor do they allow him a dispensation from the power of the vice-regent. Free choice, like merit in council, has been the result of Satan's manipulation of his followers, through faulty language, to his will. His prowess in battle is nonexistent. Could such blatant subterfuge mislead a third of the population? After twenty years of politics, Milton knew rhetoric could.

Milton's nephew tells us that Milton began the poem, years before he actually decided to write the epic, with Satan's dramatic soliloquy in book 4. Satan then was the focus and perhaps the inspiration for the poem. Satan creates the action of the poem, good and evil. As Milton conceived him, Satan is grandeur and power severed from conscience, a being who has the epic cast but not the epic soul. As we see, *Paradise Lost* gradually expounds the nature of Satan in the way an Elizabethan tragedy delineates the villain, but no Iago or Richard III has Satan's force. Milton's epic represents Milton's coming to terms with the Satan of his imagination, and we, as readers, must follow Milton's example.

The alternative to Satan may appear weak because it is more passive. The Son and Abdiel affirm that obedience to God is fulfilling. Perhaps heaven will always be a life of contemplation we here cannot imagine, Milton suggests. Few modern readers dwell on Dante's *Paradise* more than on his *Inferno*. Conflict is the heart of dramatic composition, and *Paradise Lost* is nothing if not dramatic. Milton's poem aims at happiness but can only show it through a struggle with its opposite. In literature, which must pass through time, we trace the consequences of evil. When Satan arrives in Eden at the climax of the poem, he confesses, "only in destroying I find ease" (9.129). Such is the only outlet for a nature that cannot accept its own createdness, its status as a creature created by God, but not a god himself.

The final degradation of Satan is brought about by Satan himself, not by the author's manipulation. As in a good novel, what the character does reflects what the character is. Satan elects to seduce Eve, the weaker vessel, to disguise himself as a serpent, to choose revenge over weaker creatures rather than the more heroic mode of challenging God directly again. He even degrades the literary genres of the poem by becoming the lowest of epic and tragic villains. Further, in his seduction of Eve, he degrades the language of lyric: the song of praise, by pretending to praise the Tree of the Knowledge of Good and Evil; and the love song, for his approach to Eve as in her dream is sexual. He speaks to Eve the epic equivalent of the vulgar "what's-a-nice-girl-like-you-doing-in-a-place-like-this?" Satan overheard and remembered Eve's confession of her vanity when she saw her own image in the pool. Satan was the first to split language, word versus thing, in the fall of the angels, and this degraded rhetoric characterizes him in the temptation in Eden. Rhetoric is the only way for Satan to bridge the unhealable rift between what he wishes for and what he must receive: he strives to be God and cannot succeed against God's omnipotence. But rhetoric can express what is not true, so Satan probably believes his own rhetoric, as when he doubts to himself his own statement that God created the angels (9.146–47). Ultimately Satan is left with only words, but words can kill: Eve, though she does not relinquish her free will, knowingly transgresses because she believes what the serpent tells her of the power of the Tree.

But words and things are split for the reader. At the climax of the temptation Satan hurls a series of illogicalities at Eve in order to fuddle her will by rocking her confidence: just as he, the serpent, rose in the chain of being to the level of speech, so Eve shall achieve godhead (Satan's goal) by eating of the fruit. Is God so petty he shall punish man for this tiny theft? Will he not praise her daring? Isn't it good to rise in the scale of being? What is death anyway? If the tree leads to knowledge of good, is God just to forbid it? If knowledge of evil is gained, is it not better to know and avoid the bad? Can God hurt man and still be just, still be God? Perhaps death means becoming a god? God is merely jealous and wishes to keep his knowledge. The gods derive their powers from nature, so, too, can man. Can knowledge be evil? (9.679–732).

Satan creates these thoughts for Eve, but such thoughts may run in the head of a boy pilfering an apple from a neighbor's tree or of a great hero in high tragedy deciding whether to kill his uncle for killing his father. But punishment is imminent for Eve. Satan has learned what his real weapon is, rhetoric, and has revealed himself to the reader as less than God and no true epic hero, but dangerous, like Moloch, to "less than Gods" (2.108).

In our reactions to Satan we must keep in mind the art that created him: Milton was grappling with his own creation. But the focus of the poem is the Fall. Satan is always seen in relation to that event, not as a separate force contending with God, a Christian Prometheus. Two emotions Milton wished Satan to produce in the reader's mind are wonder and anger.

SIN AND DEATH

With its strong moral polarity *Paradise Lost* divides the followers of God and the followers of Satan into good and evil, respectively, a result of Milton's use of an outmoded concept of primitive Christianity. Satan's followers comprise many consequences of their chief's behavior: Nisroch's unendurable pain, Moloch's suicidal battle philosophy, Mammon's insensitive materialism, Belial's passivity—like Dante, Milton believed that virtue was active. The only characters who develop and reappear enough to take an important part in the action are Sin and Death.

These two offspring of Satan represent in an allegorical form the consequences of Satan's surrendering his will to evil. The shift to allegory bothered Addison and some other critics, for, except for brief moments, epics do not allegorize; Homer personifies the Hours and Virgil personifies Rumor, but the main action of each poem is realistic in that the full-fledged characters act out the poem. But Sin and Death are more than allegories; they are, respectively, daughter and son, who serve at first as Satan's jailers and later as his road-builders. Death almost engages his father in battle. In these capacities they are characters in the round and not just abstractions. On the other hand, Sin sprang from Satan's forehead, like a guilty thought, was raped by Satan, and bore Death as a result. Such functions are allegory in the way that Spenser developed the allegorical romantic epic in *The Faerie Queene* and Tasso later allegorized his *Jerusalem Delivered*. Sin and Death then are only part allegory and hence do not break the level on which the action occurs. The critical objection to their presence in a pure epic seems to represent the finicky application of neoclassical rules about how epic should be written. Few readers are bothered about them today, unless they have read Addison. The action of *Paradise Lost* is so rarefied that allegory hardly breaks the action: Milton believed that Satan, God, and the Son are also metaphorical figures. In fact Sin and Death are already allegorized in the Bible: "Then when lust hath conceived, it bringeth forth sin: and sin, when it is finished, bringeth forth death" (James, 1:15).

Sin and Death have other functions as well. Their family of incest, rape, and violence stands in contrast with other families: the family of Adam and Eve, the Holy Family, and perhaps the Trinity, although Milton was not a trinitarian. The birth of Sin and Death are debased contrasts with the generation of the Son from the Father. These relationships are parodied in Sin's prayer to Satan: "Thou art my Father, thou my Author, thou" (2.864). Furthermore, they parody romance conventions; the son who unwittingly challenges his father to combat, the unmasking of the father, the lost child restored, the familial reconciliation, all derive from romance, which Milton's parody seems to challenge by reducing it to antics played out by devils. His dismissal of the genre itself comes in the invocation to book 9.

Sin and Death also unknowingly serve God by cleaning up the fruits of sin after the Fall, as the Father proclaims. Earlier in the poem, Sin held the key, "Sad instrument of all our woe" (2.872), that releases Satan from Hell. Why does Milton (or his God) give Sin a key in the first place, if Satan cannot or will not be contained? Because again and again Satan is given the opportunity of repentance, though he chooses repeatedly to recommit the sin of rebellion. The key brings into consciousness the crime of rebellion he is committing freely.

Sin and Death are allegorical, however, deliberately in name. If Milton had called them Bel and the Dragon, we would not be forced to analyze the two terms that characters and reader are asked to define: Sin and Death. They speak and deal only with Satan and transpire in his mind only. Sin is incarnate in *Paradise Lost,* and Death is foreshadowed. The reader knows what they are in their earthly forms, but not in their origins or, probably, true natures. We see them in the world but not in their pure states. Sin is the chorus hymning as well as being part of the triumph of evil: "O Parent, these are thy magnific deeds, / Thy trophies, which thou view'st as not thine own" (10.354–55). Death will devour man for his devouring of the forbidden fruit, though man will be the last of creation eaten; first, Death will feed on "Herbs, and Fruits, and Flow'rs . . . on each Beast next, and Fish, and Fowl," as Sin announces, till she seasons man, "thy last and sweetest prey" (10.603–4, 609). Milton, as often, has moved from the facts of theology to the facts of nature. Primitive man is said to have felt guilty at eating and hence killing nature. Perhaps we find the anthropological roots of original sin here. As Sin and Death become themselves, they metamorphose to pure mouths, as the Father proclaims, "My Hellhounds, to lick up the draff and filth" (10.630). With Sin and Death Milton has dramatized a philosophical essay on evil.

VI

Heaven: Hail, Holy Light

GOD

One of the problems with Satan is that Milton has isolated an almost pure evil in this one character, an absolutism we moderns often deny—although we will not name a child Satan or Adolf. Pure goodness, on the other hand, we deny totally, or we find it naive or "dippy." True, Milton would agree that human beings do not fall into such extreme characterizations, but readers trained on realistic fiction since Flaubert will find even ideal conceptions hard to accept. Yet accept we must if we are to enjoy and understand ideal poetry.

Like Satan, Milton's God arrives full of connotations, some of which were the preoccupations of Milton's religious age; others were the preoccupations of Milton himself, who was a philosopher and theologian in his own right. He belonged to the left branch of extreme Protestantism, the branch in which each worshiper sought his own credo. Rather than distinguish between Milton's beliefs and those of his age, since that controversy is now moot, I will attempt to outline in bald fashion Milton's conception of God, found in his *Christian Doctrine* and elsewhere.

Milton believed that the two necessary qualifications for religious understanding were faith and a knowledge of the Bible. He believed in no sect by the time he reached maturity. God's existence he deduced from the design of the universe; design implies a designer, who is God. But reason cannot give an account of God; for that Scripture is necessary, where the Jews also testified to God's existence. The Bible is true, but only metaphorically; it is the way God wishes us to conceive of him (The Theory of Accommodation):

> It is safest for us to form an image of God in our minds which corresponds to his representation and description of himself in the sacred writings. Admittedly, God is always described or outlined not as he really is but in such a way as will make him conceivable to us. Nevertheless, we ought to form just such a mental image of him as he, in bringing himself within the limits of our understanding, wishes us to form. Indeed he has brought himself down to our level expressly to prevent our being carried beyond the reach of human comprehension, and outside the written authority of scripture, into vague subtleties of speculation.
> (Prose, 6:133–34. translation by John Carey)

Scripture is open to all. Although the text is corrupt, a spirit guides the reader to the truth. From the Bible we can deduce attributes of God: He is wonderful and incomprehensible. The Father is separate from the Son, who is not coessential and whose power is derivative. The Holy Ghost or Spirit is an allegory of God's power. God created the world, not out of nothing, but out of himself. All substance is one and part of God. God has foreknowledge but chooses to allow free will. He chooses some for eternal life from the beginning; all others will be given a chance for salvation. God turns evil into good. Faith is not sufficient for man's salvation; man also needs good works. Faith has replaced the Law of the Old Testament. Generally, Milton applies a severe logic to scripture: Judgment Day must be symbolic, for not even God could judge the whole world in one day. God's church has no priests, no sabbath, and, typical of the age, no women.

This theology is part of Milton's God. Milton tried to create the extremes of evil and good in his poem. His creation of God presented more problems than his creation of Satan. With Satan he could rely upon stage villains for models, but no models exist for the Father. He rarely appears in the Bible, He walks on in some medieval plays, but not even Dante tried to represent Him as a character. Milton had some help from classical models: Zeus and Jupiter were believed by Renaissance thinkers to have been modeled on confused notions of the true God, so Milton's God has Olympian overtones. Michelangelo's classically heroic Christian figures showed how to combine classical sublimity and Christian doctrine in art. Moreover, the Father appeared in medieval and Renaissance art. The Father appears in glory at the opening of book 3, as if He were on a tympanum on a pilgrimage church. To such imagery Milton added a language that is pure in its austerity and clarity, unembellished by metaphor, and characterized by logic. This is Milton's way of humanizing his intellectual conception of God, for he must intellectualize Him, because the moral purpose of the poem is to "justify the ways of God to men" (1.26); from one viewpoint *Paradise Lost* is a theodicy, a justification of the ways of God, by which Milton means that responsibility for the Fall and the evil that is in the world derives from Satan and man, and not from its Creator. But as Milton knew, theological poetry can be moribund. How did Milton succeed? Did he?

Milton's argument for the justice of God's ways remains primarily a poetic one: he convinces us by the force and coherence of his poetry that what he says is imaginatively true. But the Father also uses logic: the Father created man free: that fact is crucial to the theology of the poem. The characters must demonstrate this fact in action, if not in word. The Father claims: "I form'd them free, and free they must remain, / Till they enthrall themselves" (3.124–25). God knows man shall fall and provides Redemption for him and punishment for Satan, but chooses not to interfere with the individual workings of free will. Many readers feel that God should prevent evil, but Milton's God allows it because freedom is more important than His immediate control, although He will ultimately turn evil to good through the Son's Incarnation. Whatever the Father chooses will be a limitation; if He chooses to correct the future before it occurs, characters lose their freedom; rather the Father chooses to limit His foreknowledge instead. Freedom allows men and angels to prove their obedience by each accepting the terms of obedience. Man then is tested by being forbidden to eat of the tree, as angels are tested before the fall of Satan by accepting the elevation of the Son. God does not create evil but allows it to exist. Freedom allows both men and angels the happy or the unhappy life. Without freedom, Milton believed, there is no life at all. The Father's omnipotence allows him to restrain His power. He can act or not: "my goodness, which is free / To act or not, Necessity and Chance / Approach not mee, and what I will is Fate" (7.171–73). Evil in the world is due to creatures; the good is due to God. The Father, who has been reading Milton's *Areopagitica*, asserts that "Reason also is choice" (3.108).

The Father appears a theologian, speaking the clear language of reason advocated by the Royal Society and by Francis Bacon. As in the Bible (e.g. the anger of Psalms 2:4–5), His responses are not without emotion: He is angry with Satan, pleased with the Son, and has a bitter sense of humor. Here is an example of the last:

> Only begotton Son, seest thou what rage
> Transports our adversary, whom no bounds
> Prescrib'd, no bars of Hell, nor all the chains
> Heapt on him there, nor yet the main Abyss
> Wide interrupt can hold; so bent he seems
> on desperate revenge.
> (3.80–85)

The Father can easily control Satan, if He wishes, so His ironic mockery betrays His anger and disappointment. The Father has the many emotions He has in the Bible. The emotional side of the Almighty allows Him lyric flights, where repetitions and partial repetitions of sounds create the prototype of liturgical poetry. His response to the Son's offer of sacrificing Himself sings itself, especially if read aloud:

> So Man, as is most just,
> Shall satisfy for Man, be judg'd and die,
> And dying rise, and rising with him raise

His Brethren, ransom'd with his own dear life.
So Heav'nly love shall outdo Hellish hate,
Giving to death, and dying to redeem,
So dearly to redeem what Hellish hate,
So easily destroy'd, and still destroys
In those who, when they may, accept not grace.
(3.294–302)

If the Father can hymn joy, He can likewise hymn anger in the biblical tradition. These bitter lines are spat at Sin and Death as they approach earth after the Fall, not because God is petulant, but to show His feeling for man:

I call'd and drew them thither
My Hell-hounds, to lick up the draff and filth
Which man's polluting Sin with taint had shed
On what was pure, till cramm'd and gorg'd, nigh burst
With suckt and glutted offal.
(10.629–33)

But the Father is more than the Divine Scoffer. When Adam and Eve pray, He sends down prevenient grace which anticipates their repentance, as He shall send His Son to redeem man later. The Father who is also the power behind nature provides a way for man to be happy and for Milton to illustrate that life can be worth living. Even Satan saw and was lured toward the joys of paradise for a moment before he set about wrecking it.

THE SON

The Son is also a theological idea as well as a character. His personality is not that of Christ, which He assumes only at the Incarnation, though His offer to die for man looks forward to this conception. He appears as giver of mercy, judge, warrior, and cocreator, but He does not possess these powers in Himself, but only as they are allowed by the Father. The Son is a secondary God whose divinity derives from the Father. In *Paradise Regained*, we experience the Son's development as prophet, priest, and king, but this development falls outside the action of *Paradise Lost*. The Son is created first and through Him the rest of creation. Historically, for Milton, the Old Testament was the covenant of Law; the Son as Christ opens the covenant of grace, and faith replaces law as test of obedience. In *Paradise Lost,* the Son foreshadows His role as redeemer by asking grace for man's trespass.

As a character, the Son must reflect the goodness of the Father, since goodness is unilateral in Milton's Christian world. But poetry is not theology, and in an epic poem characters must speak and act. The Son through His speech and actions proves Himself Judge and Redeemer. He is the active part of Godhead: He drives the rebel angels out of heaven and judges Adam and Eve; He also helps create the world; sets the landscape of heaven right after the War; and intercedes for man. In short, He is the parallel to and the antithesis of Satan; after Satan offers himself as voyager to earth, for example, the Son offers himself as the sacrificial corrective to the results of that voyage. The Son also is the true military hero of *Paradise Lost,* echoing Roman triumphs, which Satan fantasizes, (e.g., 10.464–65) with the words "I through the ample Air in Triumph high / Shall lead Hell Captive" (3.254–55). Hence He is the epic hero of the old heroic epics. He also completes and changes the old concept of heroism to Christian humility, as the Father points out: "in thee / Love hath abounded more than Glory abounds" (3.311–12). By such action He also proves his right to the vice-regency of heaven.

Primarily, the Son is a force for re-creation and the conversion of evil to good. As Joseph Summers noticed, the pattern at the center of the poem shows the Son replacing the hills torn up by the warring angels before he drives them out of heaven. This power of anticipation characterizes Him; His concern for good more than counterbalances his role as judge and death-sentencer. Although "Forebearance [is] no acquittance" (10.53), the Son not only offers Himself as scapegoat for man's sins but also brings to Adam and Eve the prophecy that makes their fallen lives bearable. In Genesis, the Father, not the Son, prophesies of Satan: "And I will put enmity between thee and the woman, and between thy seed and her seed; it shall bruise thy head, and thou shalt bruise his heel" (3:15). But in *Paradise Lost* the Son speaks these words, which later preserve Adam and Eve from the birth control (genocide) and suicide that they contemplate as a result of their guilt and shame. While the prophecy is an aspect of justice, it functions in the poem as mercy, too: there will be human progeny, and the forces of good will out. This is the only scrap of hope that suggests to Adam and Eve that life will be worth living in spite of pain and death. For a full understanding of the prophecy, Adam must learn from Michael that the seed is the Savior and that their struggle will not be a physical battle. Ultimately, good will triumph over evil. The Son provides psychological consolation. The Son makes his prophecy *before* He judges Adam and Eve, as He clothes them outside with animal skins and inside with the Robe of Righteousness. This last is paralleled in Isaiah (61:10) with "the garments of salvation." The Son is a constant Creator.

DEPUTY ANGELS

Michael. From a literary viewpoint, prophecy expands the action of *Paradise Lost* in a temporal dimension, just as geographical references extend it in a physical one. Michael, literally "like to God," appears as a warrior but denies the traditional glory that attaches to martial heroism:

> For in those days Might only shall be admir'd,
> And Valor and Heroic Virtue call'd;
> To overcome in Battle, and subdue
> Nations, and bring home spoils with infinite
> Man-slaughter, shall be held the highest pitch
> Of human Glory, and for Glory done
> Of triumph, to be styl'd great Conquerors,
> Patrons of Mankind, Gods, and Sons of Gods,
> Destroyers rightlier call'd and Plagues of men.
> (11.689–97)

I quote at length because Michael sums up the central attitude of the poem toward war. Milton was not a pacifist and in his *Christian Doctrine* allows war, but glory is not to be sought, nor is martial valor to be lionized; Christ brings love, not war. Yet this denial of glory is given to the most glorious of the heroic warriors. It is a clever irony that the view of human history on which the poem concludes is presented by the warrior angel, who will fight the Dragon of Revelation at the Apocalypse.

Raphael. Raphael, "God heals," assumes several roles during his long stay of four consecutive books, a third of the poem. In the Bible, he is the deliverer of Tobias in the Book of Tobit, a role Milton alludes to (4.168–72; 5.221–23) and which was common in the Renaissance; in Italy a departing son could be presented with a picture of Raphael to accompany him on a long journey. In *Paradise Lost*, Raphael combines the role of protector with that of the divine warner, wise instructor, and recapitulator of classical epic. Moreover, he helps Adam develop his speaking ability by praising him and embodies domestic aspects of Edenic society: etiquette, discourse, and lunch.

Raphael's appearance in Eden answers the narrator's prayer for a warner for Adam and Eve expressed a book earlier at Satan's entrance into Eden (4.1–7). Raphael appears as a guest, paralleling the visit of the three angels to Abraham in Genesis 18. Like them, Raphael initiates his host into aspects of spiritual life. His method, like Christ's later, is to teach by example. When he eats heartily, he shows Adam and Eve that men and angels are of the same substance; thus later, when Raphael reveals the doctrine of man's rising in the spiritual scale in order to take the place of the rebel angels, Adam has had some firsthand evidence of the doctrine. Raphael's elaboration of the doctrine of the ascent of man in the Chain of Being emerges clearly from his simile of the flower. Around this image clusters the centrality of the garden, the fruit, and the many connections between Adam and Eve and their fruitful habitat:

> O *Adam,* one Almighty is, from whom
> All things proceed, and up to him return,

If not deprav'd from good, created all
Such to perfection, one first matter all,
Indu'd with various forms, various degrees
Of substance, and in things that live, of life;
But more refin'd, more spiritous, and pure,
As nearer to him plac'd or nearer tending
Each in thir several active Spheres assign'd,
Till body up to spirit work, in bounds
Proportion'd to each kind. So from the root
Springs lighter the green stalk, from thence the leaves
More aery, last the bright consummate flow'r
Spirits odorous breathes: flow'rs and thir fruit
Man's nourishment, by gradual scale sublim'd
To vital spirits aspire, to animal,
To intellectual, give both life and sense.
Fancy and understanding, whence the Soul
Reason receives, and reason is her being,
Discursive, or Intuitive; discourse
Is oftest yours, the latter most is ours,
Differing but in degree, of kind the same.
Wonder not then, what God for you saw good
If I refuse not, but convert, as you,
To proper substance; time may come when men
With Angels may participate, and find
No inconvenient Diet, not too light Fare:
And from these corporal nutriments perhaps
Your bodies may at last turn all to spirit,
Improv'd by tract of time, and wing'd ascend
Ethereal, as wee, or may at choice
Here or in Heav'nly Paradises dwell;
If ye be found obedient, and retain
Unalterably firm to his love entire
Whose progeny you are. Meanwhile enjoy
Your fill what happiness this happy state
Can comprehend, incapable of more.
(5.469–505)

Raphael's imagery is buried in the horticultural context in which Adam and Eve live: Raphael speaks about the fruit—cf. 1.1—of a life; some fruit is forbidden; Adam and Eve are cultivators of the soil (and themselves);[23] Eve props flowers, but she herself at the Fall is the "fairest unsupported Flow'r, / From her best prop so far, and storm so nigh" (9.432–33); Adam makes a garland for Eve, while she partakes of the "root of all our woe" (9.645); Michael encourages Adam to accept death in old age as natural—"So may'st thou live, till like ripe Fruit thou drop / Into thy Mother's lap" (11.535–36); after the Fall, the Father plants grace in Adam and Eve from which spiritual renewal begins: "See Father, what first fruits on Earth are sprung / From thy implanted Grace in Man" (11.22—23); and the "Seed" of Eve (11.155), it is prophesied, will guarantee man eternal life. Such are some ways in which Raphael's symbolic interpretation of the cycle of life and death in the vegetable world are at the metaphorical root of the whole poem. Milton has embodied his theology in traditional but apt and subtle metaphors that transpose doctrine into poetry, as in the words of the Son:

> With Incense, I thy Priest before thee bring,
> Fruits of more pleasing savor from thy seed
> Sown with contrition in his heart, than those
> Which his own hand manuring all the Trees
> Of Paradise could have produc'd, ere fall'n
> From innocence.
> (11.25–30)

Raphael teaches Adam and Eve how to find truth and consolation in nature, and he teaches the reader how to feel, see, and understand the Edenic imagery in the poem. Adam must accept his return to dust, but he knows that his seed will spring forth eternal. This poetic truth sustains Adam and Eve later in the crisis after the Fall.

Raphael shows the Edenic couple what the fruits of evil are. They know that eating the forbidden fruit is wrong, but they never imagined what the results, whatever death is, would be like. From Raphael's account of the war in heaven they learn about spiritual death and the consequences of rebellion. Raphael cautions them about excess sensuality and about irrelevant curiosity. For example, he answers Adam's question about the truth between the Copernican and Ptolemaic world systems by admonishing Adam to speculate on what concerns his happiness, not mere physical data, a standard Humanist reply. Raphael also admonishes Adam and Eve to enjoy their lives in the state they are in now, although less elevated than that of angels: "Meanwhile enjoy / Your fill what happiness this happy state / Can comprehend, incapable of more" (5.503–05).

Raphael illustrates how their salvation is still in their own hands. But his teaching is mainly showing, not telling. His accounts of the war in heaven and of the Creation, which he admits are metaphors for spiritual truths Adam and Eve cannot yet comprehend, alert the reader to the symbolism of the poem and alert Adam and Eve to the dangers surrounding them. Like Michael later, Raphael takes over as secondary narrator for subjects too difficult for the human narrator. His insets are epic poems in themselves, one the traditional battle epic transformed according to Milton's Christianity and the other the epic of physics on the model of Lucretius, but transformed according to the creation story of Genesis. These are, of course, chronologically the prototypes of all others of their kind. Raphael extracts the true epic response recommended in the Renaissance, wonder: "He with his consorted *Eve* / The story heard attentive, and was fill'd / With admiration, and deep muse to hear" (7.50–52). Raphael shows Adam how to tell an epic story: with wonder and delight for the listener and with glory to the subject.

Raphael delineates the problem of writing the poem: just as Milton in *Paradise Lost* and God in the Bible felt inspired by the rightness of what they wished to say, but some system of Accommodation must translate their spiritual truths into imagery and fable apprehensible by a reader. When Adam requests Raphael to relate the story of the war in heaven, the problem for Adam is similar to that for the reader: neither have any first-hand experience of life in heaven. A Platonic duality emerges between the world as we know it and the world of the spirit, or to extend the context, to the world of art. What Raphael says of the war in heaven is true to some extent of all poetry, as are his comments on aesthetic distance:

> High matter thou injoin'st me, O prime of men,
> Sad task and hard, for how shall I relate

Heaven

> To human sense th' invisible exploits
> Of warring Spirits; how without remorse
> The ruin of so many glorious once
> And perfet while they stood; how last unfold
> The secrets of another World, perhaps
> Not lawful to reveal? yet for thy good
> This is dispens't, and what mounts the reach
> Of human sense, I shall delineate so,
> By lik'ning spiritual to corporal forms,
> As may express them best, though what if Earth
> Be but the shadow of Heav'n, and things therein
> Each to other like, more than on Earth is thought?
> (5.563–76)

Raphael's comments also ramify the concept of heroism in *Paradise Lost*. Like Michael, Raphael does not boast of martial triumphs over the rebel angels but laments the coming "arms race" as he glosses Satan's invention of gunpowder:

> yet haply of thy Race
> In future days, if Malice should abound,
> Some one intent on mischief, or inspir'd
> With dev'lish machination might devise
> Like instrument to plague the Sons of men
> For sin, on war and mutual slaughter bent.
> (6.501–6)

In contrast to Satan, Raphael understates deeds of valor through condensation: "deeds of eternal fame / Were done, but infinite" (6.240–41). His warning about seeking praise for martial valor is elaborate:

> I might relate of thousands, and thir names
> Eternize here on Earth; but those elect
> Angels contented with thir fame in Heav'n
> Seek not the praise of men; the other sort
> In might though wondrous and in Acts of War,
> Nor of Renown less eager, yet by doom
> Cancell'd from Heav'n and sacred memory,

> Nameless in dark oblivion let them dwell.
> For strength from Truth divided and from Just,
> Illaudible, naught merits but dispraise
> And ignominy, yet to glory aspires
> Vain-glorious, and through infamy seeks fame:
> Therefore Eternal silence be their doom.
> (6.373–85)

If we recall the lines in *Lycidas* relating to fame in much the same language (75–84), we may suspect an admonition to poets as well.

But Raphael's warning does not keep Eve from challenging Satan for fame. If Raphael saves Sarah and Tobias from the evil spirit Asmodeus, he has far less success with Adam and Eve. But his method is more direct. In *Tobit,* he says, "All these days I did appear unto you; but I did neither eat nor drink, but ye did see a vision" (12:19).

Like poets, all Raphael can do is warn by composing his own poem, but Raphael has taught Adam and Eve how to extract meaning, relevance, hope, and nutriment from nature and art.

Abdiel. Abdiel, who refuses to remain in Satan's camp after hearing of his intended rebellion, is Milton's representation of a "constant mind / Though single" (5.902–3). Milton returns often to this theme of the one just man in a corrupt world, a man who embodies a very biblical type of heroism. Milton underscores this symbolism by the literal meaning of his name, "Servant of God," and by his almost anonymity—he appears in the Bible only once (1 Chronicles 5:15) in an obscure genealogy. Milton's point is allegorical: any believing angel can overcome Satan, as Abdiel does easily both in debate and in combat. He personifies zeal and military action in a right cause. He also finds a parallel in the narrator, who is also alone in a fallen world, and another parallel in Christ: the proto-conception of the hero as resister to corrupt actions taken up by the body politic. It is Abdiel's strong self-reliance in his debate with Satan that enables him to triumph over his adversary when they meet on the field, "the easier conquest now / Remains" (6.37–38). Like pure zeal, Abdiel has no tact: his stroke "hung not" (6.190) in the air, for he is certain of his doctrine. In debate with Satan, he shows the same directness. He argues that Satan was created by the Son and that both the Father and Nature proclaim the Son superior. Abdiel proclaims Milton's conception that disobedience to God, the almighty power, is egoism: "Thyself not free but to thyself enthrall'd" (6.181).

Abdiel has a generic literary root as well; he is the epic malcontent, the little figure who opposes the epic hero in his mission, like Thyrsites in the *Iliad* (2.211–77) and Eurylokos in the *Odyssey* (10.251–74). Before Milton, the malcontent sometimes has valid objections to the hero's undertaking but only in *Paradise Lost* does the malcontent win over the warrior. In Milton's ironic reversal, the "hero" is Satan and the malcontent is the true hero, obedience triumphing over rebellion.

Uriel. Uriel is another angel who functions symbolically. Literally the "Fire of God" and in Milton's words "the sharpest-sighted Spirit of all in Heav'n" (3.691), Uriel fails to see through Satan's cherubic disguise, showing that hypocrisy can fool (but not damn) celestial spirits. So the narrator moralizes:

> For neither Man nor Angel can discern
> Hypocrisy, the only evil that walks
> Invisible, except to God alone,
> By his permissive will, through Heav'n and Earth:
> And oft though wisdom wake, suspicion sleeps
> At wisdom's Gate, and to simplicity
> Resigns her charge, while goodness thinks no ill
> Where no ill seems: Which now for once beguil'd
> *Uriel*, though Regent of the Sun, and held
> The sharpest-sighted Spirit of all in heav'n.
> (3.682–91).

Innocence cannot spy disguised evil; thus the Lady in *Comus* cannot see Comus's true nature disguised as a shepherd. This perception has important consequences in *Paradise Lost*, for Uriel's lack of insight helps to excuse Eve, who sees no harm in the serpent. Both Uriel and Eve know that Satan is the arch-enemy, but neither can be expected to penetrate disguises, since they both are so guileless. This deception partly exonerates Eve from complicity with Satan, but does not excuse her eating of the forbidden fruit.

Angelic Troops and Troupes. The angels at large function as guards, which shows vigilance; as warriors, which shows obedience; and as choristers, which shows gratitude. As sentinels, they man the portals of earth and Eden. While Satan slips by them, they significantly discover his presence and apprehend him. Gabriel, Ithuriel, Uzziel, and the other guards in Eden supervise and engage in epic war games. Their presence reminds Satan of his trespasses and reconfirms him in his commitment to disobedience, although at the same time offering him a chance for reconciliation with heaven. The loyal angels learn the limits of their ability to control evil: they must be ever on the watch.

Like the other characters in *Paradise Lost,* the angels learn about themselves. In the war in heaven, they at first triumph easily over Satan and his forces. But they also learn that they can experience violence, if not pain. Satan's "Gunpowder Plot" overthrows their strength momentarily; then they resort to destroying heaven by dislodging the hills and using them as missiles, until "all Heav'n / Had gone to wrack, with ruin overspread" (6.669–70, had not the Father intervened. Such is Milton's comment on the Apocalypse and the "arms race." The angels discover their own vulnerability and the futility of arms. They rediscover the need for God's protection. But both armies find they are deficient because the Chariot of Paternal Deity drives off the rebel angels at a crack. Like other Miltonic characters, the good angels learn through the trial of experience.

The angels are not creators like the Father and the Son; they cannot even re-create the landscape of heaven as the Son does before He drives down the rebels. But if they cannot create landscape, they can create art. After their fall, the rebel angels sing "Thir own Heroic deeds" (2.549), but the good angels hymn God, the source of their power—and that of the rebel angels. They do not seek epic glory for their epic achievements. When Michael downs Satan, the angels ring out "*Hosanna* to the Highest" (6.205). They improvise songs of praise on the Creation and on the offer of the Son's sacrifice as well. Their harps hang "like Quivers" (3.367) and they are aware of the paradox: here they sing the Creation in the mode of Hebrew poetry with its shifting parallelisms:

> Great are thy works, *Jehovah,* infinite
> Thy power; what thought can measure thee or tongue
> Relate thee; greater now in thy return
> Than from the Giant Angels; thee that day
> Thy thunders magnifi'd; but to create
> Is greater than created to destroy.
> Who can impair thee, mighty King, or bound
> Thy Empire? easily the proud attempt
> Of Spirits apostate and thir Counsels vain
> Thou hast repell'd, while impiously they thought
> Thee to diminish, and from thee withdraw
> The number of thy worshippers. Who seeks
> To lessen thee, against his purpose serves
> To manifest the more thy might: his evil
> Thou usest, and from thence creat'st more good.
> Witness this new-made World, another Heav'n
> From Heaven Gate not far, founded in view
> On the clear *Hyaline,* the Glassy Sea;
> Of amplitude almost immense, with Stars
> Numerous, and every Star perhaps a World
> Of destin'd habitation; but thou know'st
> Thir seasons: among these the seat of men,
> Earth with her nether ocean circumfus'd,
> Thir pleasant dwelling-place. Thrice happy men,
> And sons of men, whom God hath thus advanc't,
> Created in his Image, there to dwell
> And worship him, and in reward to rule
> Over his Works, on Earth, in Sea, or Air,
> And multiply a Race of Worshippers
> Holy and just: thrice happy if they know
> Thir happiness, and persevere upright.
> (7.602–32)

Chronologically, here is the origin of psalm, prophecy, and lyric poetry. God creates; angels reflect.

VII

Eden: Never Since Met Such

NATURAL GRATITUDE: THE LOVELIEST PAIR

The difficulties Milton faced in creating his prelapsarian couple were similar but more complex than those he faced when creating his godhead. God is a remote ideal; but human perfection is denied everywhere. Moreover, the modern reader must accept the seventeenth-century attitude that women are second to men, a hierarchical attitude advocated by the Bible itself: "But I would have you know, that the head of every man is Christ; and the head of the woman is the man; and the head of Christ is God" (I Corinthians 11:3). But Milton's treatment of Eve transcends this doctrine, so that Eve, as we shall see, emerges as the greatest epic heroine.

Happiness is usually a static and undramatic quality difficult to render into literature, an art that moves through time and moves us through dramatic conflict. The Renaissance painter could place his Adam and Eve, or his saints, in a symbolic and attractive landscape. His characters could communicate through the *sacra coversazione* or sacred conversation, a silent interchange and purely spiritual communication. But poetry is not visual in the same way. Characters must be described in words, and in an epic must speak and act. Milton solves this problem of the stasis of innocence by his active concept of innocence. Far from perfect, Adam and Eve must shape their nature as they shape the garden. They are happy, but in the Aristotelian sense of being active on behalf of someone else (e.g. *Ethics,* 1169a), in this case on behalf of each other, of God, and of the future human race. Their happiness is also contingent upon keeping God's sole commandment not to eat of the fruit of the Tree of the Knowledge of Good and Evil.

Unlike characters in a realistic novel, Milton's couple are the ideal toward which cosmetics, barbells, universities, and charm schools feebly tend. They are beautiful, spontaneously intelligent, loving, gracious in speech, in harmony with their environment, mutually satisfying in sex, and natural poets. Even Satan praises and envies their state. They are naked and guiltless. In their Protestant paradise, they work—but not laboriously. Their lives have meaning because they have unrealized goals, for instance, to rise in the hierarchy of being to a more spiritual state, to say nothing of their aspirations for their progeny. But their progress is assured if they obey, so their future is under their own control. Their world is expressed perfectly by their speech, their formal conversations implying mutual respect and natural gratitude. Adam's opening words are addressed to Eve:

> Sole partner and sole part of all these joys,
> Dearer thyself than all; needs must the Power
> That made us, and for us this ample World
> Be infinitely good, and of his good
> As liberal and free as infinite,
> That rais'd us from the dust and plac't us here
> In all this happiness.
> (4.411–17)

The speech of Eden is praise, praise for each other, for the garden, for God. If the language sounds formal and remote, that is Milton's point. How do people speak when they are perfectly happy? We don't know, but in Milton's mind their elevated language shows that they have more dignity than we presently allow. At a dinner party or in a film, Adam and Eve would sound absurdly pretentious. But in Eden their language fits.

Speech is spontaneous, as in Adam's naming the animals, but other intellectual disciplines must be learned through physical work and through conversation with each other and with divinities. The conversations in Eden include as topics psychology, philosophy—both in the practical sense of behavior and in the abstract sense of metaphysics—astronomy, gardening, ethics, animal behavior, music, and the one prohibition. From Raphael they learn about their spiritual natures, angelology, history (the war in heaven and Creation), the Chain of Being, the limits of intellectual curiosity—it should end when human happiness becomes irrelevant—and the dangers of lust. After the Fall, Adam and Eve become more dependent upon each other's now-fallen abilities, as they discuss the more painful topics of suicide, birth control, and death. In a literary sense, they inhabit the pastoral world of contemplation and conversation and also the georgic world of work, both before and after the Fall. Throughout all these discussions, Milton's concern with dialogue and debate illustrates his early intellectual training: he believed that talk educates, that rhetoric can be a force for human development.

Milton's ideas can be traced to sources, as everyone's can, but Milton thoroughly assimilated these ideas, made them his own, and also turned them into poetry. Far from mere insets in the epic, the ideas grow out of the action. When in book 5 Eve wakes from the dream created by Satan, she feels guilty. In order to relieve her anxiety, Adam expatiates on a theory close to Freud's: the matter of dreams is a residue of memory, which, when our censoring apparatus—Milton's reason and Freud's superego—is inoperative, fancy creates by reassembling facts in a nonlogical way in order to express our fears and desires. All have desires forbidden by society; only through action, when the will accedes to these desires in our conscious mind, can crime occur. In Freud's system, of course, evil has only the meaning something contrary to society's wishes, but I am abstracting here to illustrate the common ground beneath the two systems. The distinction between desire and act is crucial to both systems: fantasy and act are different. One is ostracized or otherwise punished, at least in a non-neurotic society, not for fantasies but for actions. In *Paradise Lost,* the ideal of behavior is a will that is strong enough to control appetite, to control even reason, if reason should go astray. This is only one small example of how the major problems of human life enter in Milton's epic, in ways that illustrate and clarify them.

Another focal discussion is the question of the Ptolemaic versus the Copernican system of the universe—whether the sun revolves around the earth or the reverse. This question was still open and alive in Milton's day. Milton had visited Galileo, held under house arrest because he had championed Copernicus's view. Adam and Eve celebrate the stars and planets in their hymns, for both are curious. From Adam and Eve we learn that such curiosity is natural, even a means of attaining perfection, as Raphael suggests. What limits human curiosity for Milton and other Renaissance humanists is its relevance to human happiness: intellect must serve humanity, not the reverse. The purpose of life is not to be scholarly, which can clearly be an irrelevant vanity, but to be happy. Happiness can be fed by knowledge but only to the point, in Milton's view, that it is conducive to human well-being. Happiness is not an abstract question for Milton. When Eve asks why the stars come out at night when no one is there to see them, her question has relevance. She expects an answer because God has a purpose in everything—or, as we would say, everything has a cause. Adam answers, rather dubiously in retrospect, that starlight keeps Night from gaining back his old rule, provides energy to plants (maybe it does?), and presents a beautiful object for angels to hymn as they wander the earth in darkness. If Adam's answers are slightly makeshift, they approve Eve's question: his answer is conducive to Eve's happiness, in that it extends her appreciation of nature. Intellect can be beneficial—would that Eve had questioned why the serpent bothered to tell her that he ate the fruit and gained the gift of speech. Adam's answers are not meant to be definitive, of course, but they are based partly upon observed phenomena; such as the singing of the angelic choruses Adam and Eve hear in Eden. He turns fact into the wisdom of humility: we are not the only creatures who benefit from God's creation. Such knowledge is potentially a benefit, for Eve has a possible reply to Satan's claim in her dream that the moon sets the world's beauty "in vain, / If none regard" (5.43–44). Milton's Eden contained the seeds of human happiness, just as it contained all the types of fruit now dispersed throughout the world.

But Raphael teaches Adam the restraints on the pursuit of knowledge. Adam must learn that the end of all knowledge is admiration and praise. Adam's question about the two astronomical systems brings a mild rebuke from Raphael, that nature is not always to be fathomed by human intelligence:

> Heav'n is for thee too high
> To know what passes there; be lowly wise:
> Think only what concerns thee and thy being;
> Dream not of other Worlds.
> (8.172–75)

Adam, for prelapsarian intelligences need only a hint to understand and expand truth, develops Raphael's ideas in light of his earlier psychology:

> But apt the Mind or Fancy is to rove
> Uncheckt, of her roving is no end;
> Till warn'd, or by experience taught, she learn
> That not to know at large of things remote
> From use, obscure and subtle, but to know
> That which before us lies in daily life,
> Is the prime Wisdom; what is more, is fume,
> Or emptiness, or fond impertinence,
> And renders us in things that most concern
> Unpractic'd, unprepar'd, and still to seek.
> (8.188–97)

Since Adam has learned from Raphael's account of the war in heaven that history and poetry have a purpose, he uses the above remarks for his own presentation of an autobiography, the first such.

Eden

While Adam does not try to educate Raphael, he shows the angel that he can extrapolate what is relevant from his own history. In strong contrast to Satan's distortion of autobiographical fact, Adam constructs a true story, though "to tell how human Life began / Is hard; for who himself beginning knew?" (8.250–51). His words echo Satan's (5.855–64).

Through Adam's account of his beginnings, we see into Milton's conception of the natural human being. By instinct, immediately after his birth, Adam wishes to stand erect and observes the world around him. He makes an emotional assessment of it: the world is happy. Then, like a baby, he observes himself, walks, then runs. He has no knowledge of who he is or what caused him, though he naturally deduces the categories of self and cause. He finds speech natural and could name "Whate'er I saw" (8.273). Adam questions hills, rivers, woods, plains, and other natural sights about his creation in order to praise his creator in a fit of natural gratitude. He deduces that his maker is a superior force since he himself cannot create. Adam then has the first dream, a vision of Eden, almost allegorically showing the origins of the perfect place; the land in which he is created is not paradise but a land he shall be banished back to after the Fall and so creates a cushion for the Expulsion later. What is significant at this point is that man naturally dreams about a paradise that does exist. Adam's origins reflect not only childhood but the development of the human race: God checks Adam's wandering nomadic tendencies by rooting him in the garden of Eden to till the soil, just as the race gravitated to the neolithic village and farming, yielding up its more adventurous wanderings. Unfortunately, these impulses will be reactivated somewhat after the Fall, but the dream of a perfect place where wandering shall cease will be still the dream.

Adam needs divine guidance, then, shortly after he is born. As in Milton's *Christian Doctrine,* man deduces God the Maker from His creation. But whereas fallen human beings must garner wisdom from the Bible, Adam learns by debating directly with God. This confrontation puts the divine imprimatur on rhetoric as a learning tool: the Father even baits Adam to goad him to work out his position in the divine scheme and to learn what a human being is. Unfallen Adam assumes that he has a right to be happy. While naming the animals, he presumably notices their pairing and then asks God for a mate. To try him, God suggests that perhaps a member of the animal kingdom would do. Adam after all does know their language. Adam then reasons that he is superior to an animal, and, when God suggests His Own solitude as a model of self-sufficiency, Adam reasons that he is not God either. In an ironic way, Adam is reasoning toward his Fall and redemption, since Eve is instrumental in both these events. More to the immediate point, he is learning about mutual human need and dependence, and even feeling the roots of generation stirring. Through a combination of induction, deduction, and imagination, Adam posits that companionship must be mutual, a "rational delight" (8.391), among equals alike in nature, within the limits set by seventeenth-century male chauvinism. Further, a helpmeet will solace his defects. Although Adam deduces the necessity of a mate also from God's promise of a race of descendants, Adam learns from the animal world and from God's behavior toward him that "Collateral love, and dearest amity" (8.426) are necessary for happiness, not mere lust.

Having won the right to a mate by using reason, observing his surroundings, and persevering with God, Adam now has a second vision. The first showed the perfect place; the second now reveals the perfect woman. Both materialize. God told Adam that Eden was contingent; now he finds out that Eve is: he must coax her away from her natural self-love to become his wife and the mother of the human race. Adam shows a predisposition to blame his Creator for his faults when he maintains that Eve's beauty "*Seems*" (8.550) the sum of earthly bliss. Raphael warns him that sex and beauty can corrupt, though "Love refines / The thoughts, and heart enlarges" (8.589-90). Adam's reply that Eve's graces "subject not" (8.607) shows that he grasps the distinction between impulse and act, although the will fails to check the former at his Fall. But Adam has learned how self-sufficient he is and can be. His wishes have been granted, and he has the moral education to withstand temptation. His will is free; through love he can ascend to the status of an angel or fall to the level we act on.

Eden

Eve, too, has an independent development. She admits Adam's authority in a way to make modern feminists cringe:

> O thou for whom
> And from whom I was form'd flesh of thy flesh,
> And without whom am to no end, my Guide
> And Head.
> (4.440–43)

But no previous epic heroine has such central importance. Eve develops morally and intellectually to play a separate part in their tragedy and redemption. She is in one sense the true human hero of the whole poem, for she eventually saves Adam, just as Christ saves their posterity. Milton compares her to classical deities (e.g., 5.380–83), though she is fairer. Her closest classical parallel is Helen of Troy, the catalyst for the fall of that city (also brought down by an apple of discord). But Homer's Helen remains a pawn compared to Eve, who actively and before our eyes brings about Fall and salvation.

Milton's first depiction of Eve presents her frankly as sexual companion intended to attract Adam to produce us: "For softness shee and sweet attractive Grace" (4.298):

> Shee as a veil down to the slender waist
> Her unadorned golden tresses wore
> Dishevell'd, but in wanton ringlets wav'd
> As the Vine curls her tendrils, which impli'd
> Subjection, but requir'd with gentle sway,
> And by her yielded, by him best receiv'd,
> Yielded with coy submission, modest pride
> And sweet reluctant amorous delay.
> (4.304–11)

Walter Savage Landor once said he would rather have written the last two lines than all the poetry written since Milton's time.[24] Even if we disagree with Milton, the power of his poetry can sweep us away. Yet content counts here too: the purpose of Eden, like other famous gardens in literature, is procreation. Puritans were not necessarily prudes, and Milton's lash against the latter, those who would exclude sex from the perfect paradise, is worth retailing in full:

> Nor those mysterious parts were then conceal'd,
> Then was not guilty shame: dishonest shame
> Of Nature's works, honor dishonorable,
> Sin-bred, how have ye troubl'd all mankind
> With shows instead, mere shows of seeming pure,
> And banisht from man's life his happiest life,
> Simplicity and spotless innocence.
> So pass'd they naked on, nor shunn'd the sight
> Of God or Angel, for they thought no ill:
> So hand in hand they pass'd, the loveliest pair
> That ever since in love's embraces met.
> (4.312–22)

Adam and Eve's inequality accounts for some of their compatibility in Milton's view. If love and lust can be sundered now and sex is often not without guilt, it remains pure in itself:

> Whatever Hypocrites austerely talk
> Of Purity and place and innocence,
> Defaming as impure what God declares
> Pure, and commands to some, leaves free to all.
> Our Maker bids increase, who bids abstain
> But our Destroyer, foe to God and Man?
> (4.744–49)

To Adam and Eve abstinence is out of the question.

Eve's role as partner is more than sexual, of course; she and Adam discourse over the range of intellectual subjects listed above, and later she is not afraid to contradict him. Even in her role of love companion, she invents the love elegy. Her composition takes the usual course of thought and metaphor in Eden: an extrapolation from nature to idea, as in their hymns. Eve's poem is a meditation on the beauties of nature and then a demotion of these beauties in the name of love. The rhe-

torical nature of the lyric—in form it is an elaborate catalogue repeated with climactic variation—emphasizes the triumph of the
human over the natural, of art over nature, of companionship over
solitude. The first love lyric is an intricate garland:

> With thee conversing I forget all time,
> All seasons and thir change, all please alike.
> Sweet is the breath of morn, her rising sweet,
> With charm of earliest Birds; pleasant the Sun
> When first on this delightful Land he spreads
> His orient Beams, on herb, tree, fruit, and flow'r,
> Glist'ring with dew; fragrant the fertile earth
> After soft showers; and sweet the coming on
> Of grateful Ev'ning mild, then silent Night
> With this her solemn Bird and this fair Moon,
> And these the Gems of Heav'n, her starry train:
> But neither breath of Morn when she ascends
> With charm of earliest Birds, nor rising Sun
> On this delightful land, nor herb, fruit, flow'r,
> Glist'ring with dew, nor fragrance after showers,
> Nor grateful Ev'ning mild, nor silent Night
> With this her solemn Bird, nor walk by Moon,
> Or glittering Star-light without thee is sweet.
> (4.639–56)

The repetitions of the poem point to the deep and obsessive feeling
behind Eve's lyric. The fact that it is a prologue to her question about
the stars shows how natural and spontaneous her expression is. This
is the most elaborate poem about human love in *Paradise Lost,* and
significantly Milton gives it to Eve, the saver of humanity. The intellectual framework of the poem underscores her intelligence, the intelligence that if she does not want to hear Raphael's story firsthand does
not mean that her desire to listen to it later, as affectionately told by
Adam, makes her any less intellectual. The theme that love triumphs
over nature and time—note the chronological sequences in the lyric—
is relevant to the whole epic.

Eve's lyric is also a reaffirmation of her commitment to Adam, who had to woo her with gentle force from her own reflection in the pool. Quite naturally Eve is attracted by her own image in the pool. Unlike Narcissus, however, her action is not destructive or even evil (only eating the fruit of the tree is that). Adam convinces Eve that he is her source, an analogy with Adam's seeking after his Maker. When she relents and becomes Adam's mate, it is because truth and gratitude have conquered beauty, truth being the higher good; the whole sequence represents a process of maturation. But overcoming one's vanity in action does not mean obliterating the inclination. Like Adam's attraction to Eve, which can become uxorious if let out of control, so Eve's attraction to herself remains the weakness through which to test her character. Sex and self-love can lead to destruction in more places than just Eden. But her poem shows the harmony that can live in spite of such weaknesses, a harmony of "Taste, Sight, Herbs, Fruits, and Flow'rs, / Walks, and the melody of Birds" (8.527–28).

FALL

From this height of happiness Milton must make plausible the Fall. Satan, when he first appears in *Paradise Lost,* is already fallen, but Adam and Eve are within their sphere perfect, though perfectible to higher realms of spirituality. In both falls, Milton must demonstrate that the sinner is responsible at least in part for the sin. In order to be morally convincing in his account of the Fall in Eden, Milton must employ a believable psychology: Adam and Eve must maintain their free will, though they are weakened by Satan's strategies. Hence they qualify for Aristotle's definition of tragic heroes (*Poetics,* 1453a). Unless they can be faulted, they cannot be punished; unless they can be partly undermined, they cannot be given grace. Furthermore, if God's foreknowledge of the Fall had prevented it, then there would be no free will:

> . . . many there be that complain of divin Providence for suffering *Adam* to transgresse, foolish tongues! when God gave him reason, he gave him freedom to choose, for reason is but choosing; he had

bin else a meer artificiall *Adam*, such an *Adam* as he is in the mo-
tions [puppet shows]. We our selves esteem not of that obedience,
or love, or gift, which is of force: God therefore left him free, set
before him a provoking object, ever almost in his eyes; herein con-
sisted his merit, herein the right of his reward, the praise of his
abstinence. (Prose, 2:527)

A stumbling block here is not accepting the psychological fact that we,
before and after the Fall, can will an action for immediate pleasure
that we know in the long run is wrong. To think "To hell with the
consequences" might find ourselves there.

Adam and Eve must know that they are doing wrong in eating
the fruit of the garden. Where do they get a knowledge of good and
evil? Milton tells us in his *Areopagitica* (Prose, 2:514–17) that postlapsarian man knows good only by knowing evil. If such were true for
Adam and Eve, the Fall would be the only track to experience and to
eternal life. But before the Fall, humanity can know good by means of
firsthand experience and evil through the imagination. God tells them
that eating the fruit is evil and so is its result, death. Raphael dramatizes in human terms the evil of the war in heaven. The crisis of *Paradise Lost* comes when Adam and Eve experience a conflict between
what they know is wrong—eating the fruit—and what they desire, to
satisfy their passions. Knowingly, they elevate desire over reason. We
know that if their passions are strong, their intellects are strong as
well. Milton does not share the romantic conception of the omnipotence of passion, especially in Eden. He believes that Adam and Eve
freely choose to give in, though not without many extenuating circumstances that weakened, but did not destroy, their will. The question is
always an important one: how much is any individual responsible for
what he does? Politics, law, course grades, and individual relationships, among other areas, are affected by our attitude toward this
question. Our more subjective age might be more lenient than Milton's, but he delves deep into our actions, as Adam and Eve find themselves immersed in the bickering circumstances that test their character
and produce their tragedy. An epic poet must deal with such questions
concretely.

When the narrator signals in his invocation to book 9 that tragedy is about to emerge, the reader is hardly surprised: from the title
on, the reader has been anticipating the Fall. Even Milton's descriptions of paradise hint at future gloom:

> . . . Not that fair field
> Of *Enna,* where *Proserpin* gath'ring flow'rs
> Herself a fairer Flow'r by gloomy *Dis*
> Was gather'd, which cost *Ceres* all that pain
> To seek her through the world . . . . .
> . . . . . .
> . . . . . might with this Paradise
> Of *Eden* strive.
> (4.268–72; 274–75)

In book 9, the archetypal villain, Dis (Pluto) himself, breaks into
paradise to destroy it. And other crises arise to entangle human passions further.

The major crisis, however, is the marital dispute, which weakens
the defenses of both Adam and Eve, so that Satan finds them at their
weakest moment. The dispute itself is brought about by another minor
crisis: the growing garden whose luxuriousness is both a symbol and
a condition of their difficulty. Running a quick time-and-motion study
on the problem, Eve determines that affection interferes with cultivat-
ing the garden; therefore they should work separately. She is not being
the primal yuppie in this reaction—the garden is expanding and their
job is to control its luxuriance. So far her conclusion is logical, since
reason controls her action.

Adam goes a step further and creates a hierarchy of needs: what
Eve suggests is true, but they are threatened by an adversary who has
seduced angels. The work will be aided by their future offspring. His
method is that of the city police: in order to prevent a crime, remove
the victim from the possible scene.

Passion begins to rule when Eve takes the suggestion personally:

> Offspring of Heav'n and Earth, and all Earth's Lord,
> That such an Enemy we have, who seeks

> Our ruin, both by thee inform'd I learn,
> And from the parting Angel over-heard
> As in shady-nook I stood behind,
> Just then return'd at shut of Ev'ning Flow'rs.
> But that thou shouldst my firmness therefore doubt
> To God or thee, because we have a foe
> May tempt it, I expected not to hear.
> (9.273–281)

One can pinpoint in this passage the shift from reason to passion (9.279). For the first time, serious conflict enters Eden. Earlier, Eve could be won to the marriage bower partly because it did not conflict with her vanity (or Adam's). Her *f*-sounds that follow suggest tears: "His fraud is then thy fear, which plain infers / Thy equal fear that my firm Faith and Love / Can by his fraud be shak'n or seduc't" (9.285–87). Trouble occurs when neurosis meets neurosis. Adam, too, resorts to an emotional response. If Eve's vanity is piqued because she feels that Adam is deprecating her strength, Adam's uxoriousness is wakened at the thought that Eve is growing away from him somehow and that she is not taking his authority. Behind this passage is Aristotle's old distinction between vanity and love: love is wanting good for the sake of the beloved, not the self, the desire for which is vanity. At this moment of crisis, both recede into their own cells, nursing imagined offenses. We must keep in mind that such bickering, so universal now, is not sin in Eden, whose morality rests on one simple prohibition. Though not sinning, such scenes can create disaster, when reason breaks its mooring. So Adam's response that temptation casts suspicions upon the one tempted is clearly nonsense, even if he never read *Paradise Regained*. His answer is meant to help him regain his authority by force, since he is now abandoning reason. Quite rightly Adam deduces danger, but his methods are too patently the result of his passions. If Adam wobbles, he quickly regains solid ground by emphasizing his weakness and the help Eve can provide by being near him. But he does not directly assuage Eve's wound.

Eve retorts by defining paradise as a place where they can repel their foes, else there is limitation on their freedom and paradise is not a true paradise. She argues Milton's case in *Areopagitica*, that virtue must be tested, but that argument is for fallen man, who cannot know good without confronting evil. Eve, like Adam, does not lose all rational control; she points out to Adam that temptation is no dishonor. But she bridles too much at the thought of being vulnerable, almost at their happiness being contingent at all, by punning on the Hebrew meaning of *Eden* (pleasure): "Frail is our happiness, if this be so, / And *Eden* were no *Eden* thus expos'd" (9.340–41).

If Eve becomes more philosophical, so does Adam. Resorting to his psychology of book 5, Adam explains in a Socratic vein that the only way to sin is to elevate some other good over obedience to God's commandment. Adam argues that reason will mistakenly misinform the will, that is, turn it toward a lesser or seeming good. Adam imagines the Fall with true clairvoyance, but he yields to pacifying Eve's aroused vanity by supplying her with a reason for their separation that she had not thought of. Knowing she wishes to separate their work, Adam contradicts Aristotle's dictum and assuages his own fearful ego: he does not keep persuading Eve, though he realizes she has not yet broken away and does not even wait for her reply to his words. Against his best judgment, he releases her, suddenly abandoning reason altogether, completely and for the first time. The shift is dramatic: "But if thou think, trial unsought may find / Us both securer than thus warn'd thou seem'st, / Go; for thy stay, not free, absents thee more" (9.370–72). Ironically Adam does just what he has described as the route to sin: elevated a lesser good over a higher; rather than Eve's safety, he puts his own peace of mind first. As Adam told Raphael, wisdom in Eve's presence sometimes falls degraded. Adam risks Eve for a morning's peace of mind. He knows that she has imagined the Fall incorrectly: she surmises that Satan would not attack her alone because honor would drive him to try Adam, the greater warrior. Satan, as we learn later, was hoping to find Eve alone (9.421–22). Neither has yet fallen (cf. e.g., 9.659), but their defenses have been weakened by separation and by domestic strife. Reason has lost a foothold.

Eve's fall is further mitigated. It results from a mixture of vanity and reason. She knows that Satan's flattery is just that but seems to enjoy it anyway. Unacquainted with metamorphosis or hypocrisy, she assumes the serpent is not to be suspected of lying—when did an animal lie before? (Adam knows the language of animals.) Furthermore, then, reason suggests that, if the serpent gained human speech from the forbidden tree and if he did not die, why should Adam and Eve? The very fact that the tree is forbidden makes it attractive; it is also lunch time. Eve feels the tree may release her from her position of being subservient to Adam, and even elevate her to the divine status alluded to by Satan. Her intellect, however, is not deceived: she repeats to Satan and to herself the sole commandment. The self-aggrandizement that lured her to marvel at her reflected face in the pool, that caused her to wish to combat Satan alone in order to gain glory, dares her now to eat of the Tree. In short, she gambles with Cavalier recklessness that the experience gained from eating of the Tree, the good Satan promises, may be greater than any good she has in Eden. Through the logical fallacy of composition, she deduces that the serpent did not die by eating of the Tree, and that therefore she will not die (by this logic the food of the dung beetle would be good for us):

> For us alone
> Was death invented? or to us deni'd
> This intellectual food, for beasts reserv'd?
> For Beasts it seems: yet that one Beast which first
> Hath tasted, envies not, but brings with joy
> The good befall'n him, Author unsuspect,
> Friendly to man, far from deceit or guile.
> What fear I then, rather what know to fear
> Under this ignorance of Good and Evil,
> Of God or Death, of Law or Penalty?
> Here grows the Cure of all, this Fruit Divine,
> Fair to the Eye, inviting to the Taste,
> Of virtue to make wise: what hinders then
> To reach, and feed at once both Body and Mind?
> (9.766–79)

So we talk to ourselves when we want something we shouldn't. She misinforms her will of the good—in this case experience—she will gain from the trespass. Her faulty reason assumes that what one knows is the limit one can suffer. In the *Christian Doctrine,* Milton outlines that Fall from another perspective, including what Eve has left out of her reasoning:

> For what fault is there which man did not commit in committing this sin? He was to be condemned both for trusting Satan and for not trusting God; he was faithless, ungrateful, disobedient, greedy, uxorious; she, negligent of her husband's welfare; both of them committed theft, robbery with violence, murder against their children (i.e., the whole human race); each was sacrilegious and deceitful, cunningly aspiring to divinity although thoroughly unworthy of it, proud and arrogant. (Prose, 6:383–84; translation by John Carey)

On another level, Eve's action is a parody of the true epic hero who knows he is risking death but risks it anyway for fame and his people. Epic heroes usually confront death consciously and with a full knowledge of what death means. Achilles, Odysseus, Aeneas, Beowulf, and other heroes defy death directly, though they know they may die in old age but probably will die in battle; that is the nature of the old epic heroism. Satan pretends to such heroism and does take the risk of battle and of espionage, but Eve risks her life—and ours—out of guesswork and without sure gain in mind. Moreover she acts solely for herself, without observing her Satanic parallels.

After the Fall, infernal resemblances increase. Like Satan, she does homage to the Tree, rather than to its Creator; she promises the plant matins replacing those songs she and Adam sang in the morning. Rather than a nurturer of plants, she has become a slave to one. She assumes Satan's position, that to be less than first in the hierarchy is to be without freedom. She assumes Belial's rationalization that perhaps God will ignore her sin and punishment. She falls to Mammon's level, believing that falling is fun and that its fruits can be enjoyed. Finally she assumes Satan's desperate course that others must suffer, if she is to suffer, and determines to drag Adam into her fate, out of jealousy. To Adam, she silently passes over her fears that death may ensue; the only fear she expresses to him is that she may rise in the scale of being beyond his company, a sure-fire stimulus to his uxoriousness. She praises serpent and fruit, herself playing Satan's role as tempter, craftily assessing her prey's weakness. In all sincerity, she praises Adam's fall as the result of love, actually the result of being so fearful of losing her that he commits what he rightly believes is suicide. The real meaning of love, wishing the best for someone else for that person's sake, lies in the future, when Eve sheds her serpentine skin.

Adam, too, parodies true heroism. Like a real hero, he falls with full knowledge of his sinning. He knows when Eve appears that her flushed face signals shame. His justification is helplessness:

> So forcible within my heart I feel
> The Bond of Nature draw me to my own,
> My own in thee, for what thou art is mine;
> Our State cannot be sever'd, we are one,
> One Flesh; to lose thee were to lose myself.
> (9.955–59)

The bond of nature could also draw Adam to ask God's forgiveness for Eve or even to offer himself for her, but he acts rashly, trusting in God's mercy after the Fall not to destroy whom he has created, wreck nature, or give Satan a rhetorical advantage in enabling him to say that God is fickle and ruins His creatures. Adam is partly right: God will not destroy creation, but he is also partly wrong: God has not destroyed paradise, he himself has. Epic heroes offer themselves to death, but not because their ladies are doomed. His action, like Eve's, is not based on a political act, self-sacrifice for his people, but weakness and the very opposite of political action. Adam, too, gambles on God's mercy against his judgment, as epic heroism dwindles to domestic tragedy. If Adam and Eve were aware of the enormity of their punishment, their action would be, in retrospect, more grand. But it is in their suffering that their greatest trials come and are partially surmounted.

AFTERMATH

Like all humanity, Adam and Eve have to learn what death is, but they learn it for the first time. It involves a complex process of rejection of the idea, awareness, acceptance, and letting-go. They experience our difficulty in accepting the naturalness of death. As in childhood, in Eden they are hoodwinked into believing time stands still, until they are strong enough to support the idea. God's grace helps Adam and Eve realize that death has phases, chronologically outlined by Milton in his *Christian Doctrine* as follows:

I. The evils which lead to death: guilt and terrors of conscience.

II. Spiritual death. Loss of God's grace, right reason, righteousness, liberty to do good. One becomes a slave to evil. The will dies.

III. The death of the body, spirit, and soul.

IV. Last Judgment: possible eternal death. (Prose, 6:393–98)

As Adam and Eve begin to understand what death in these four stages means, the reader senses that the poem passes into another world. Of all the climaxes in literature, that of *Paradise Lost* is most unmistakable. On the narrative level, the characters shift from happiness to despair. On the generic level, the epic shifts to tragedy. The intellectual dialogues, the love song, and the hymns that Adam and Eve composed earlier now become soliloquies of lament and complaint. The duet disappears. Language itself falls; the formal patterns of address, reminiscent of heavenly language and emblematic of man's conception of himself, also disappear. Note the earlier formality of address and the elevated diction: "Best Image of myself and dearer half, / The trouble of thy thoughts this night in sleep / Affects me equally" (5.95–97). After the Fall, language comes closer to what is overheard at the supermarket. Note the bad pun: "O *Eve*, in evil hour thou didst give ear / To that false Worm" (9.1067–68). Nature, too, falls in the wrenching of the solar system off its axis, producing seasonal changes. The serpent is punished by being forced to crawl on its belly and eat the dust, symbolic of the fall of all nature. Animals prey upon each other. Death and pain enter the world. Carried away with the greatest event in history, the blind narrator, fallen on evil days himself, breaks through the aesthetic distance between himself and his characters and exclaims in a poignant apostrophe, as if he were there when Eve separates from Adam:

> O much deceiv'd, much failing, hapless *Eve,*
> Of thy presum'd return! event perverse!
> Thou never from that hour in Paradise
> Found'st either sweet repast, or sound repose;
> Such ambush hid among sweet Flow'rs and Shades.
> (9.404–8)

The first result of the Fall is an intoxication with the freedom of sinning—the high of the murderer. Then exhilaration yields to the hangover, guilt. Adam and Eve now resort, like Belial, to hiding themselves and hiding their evident shame at breaking contract. The impulse to bury themselves in clothes, as they sense their nakedness, or to bury themselves in earth, since they unconsciously wish for death, takes them over: "Cover me ye Pines, / Ye Cedars, with innumerable boughs / Hide me" (9.1088–90). Adam and Eve now share our world of experiencing evil but imagining and yearning for good. They know what they have done wrong—their descendants are less sure—and are tormented by conscience. Guilt is universal after the Fall: the narrator notes how Columbus found the Indian almost naked but covering his shame. This sense of shame is only part of man's loss of control over his passions. He no longer feels able to control and harmonize thought and feeling. The outer world of Eden reflects this inner world of tumult, symbolized by winds, once the image of Edenic harmony (see 4.264–66):

> . . . high Winds worse within
> Began to rise, high Passions, Anger, Hate,
> Mistrust, Suspicion, Discord, and shook sore
> Thir inward State of Mind, calm Region once
> And full of Peace, now toss't and turbulent:
> For Understanding rul'd not, and the Will
> Heard not her lore, both in subjection now
> To sensual Appetite, who from beneath
> Usurping over sovran Reason claim'd
> Superior sway.
> (9.1122–31)

Inner conflict seeks expression without, so Adam and Eve assault each other. Adam becomes the first misogynist

> Thus it shall befall
> Him who to worth in Woman overtrusting
> Lets her Will rule; restraint she will not brook,
> And left to herself, if evil thence ensue,
> Shee first his weak indulgence will accuse.
> (9.1182–86)

As it is easier to blame a whole sex or race than to accept one's guilt, Adam blames his uxoriousness on Eve; lying to himself, he claims among other nonsense that he thought her beauty proof against evil. The argument between Adam and Eve, like much human bickering, is obsessed with cause, and hence blame. What caused the Fall? Eve's separation? Adam's permission? Is this what I get for all I did for you? You made me do it. . . . "Neither self-condemning" (9.1188), adds the narrator, pointing to the first step in their coming rehabilitation.

Unlike Eve, Adam continues to fall. At the judgment, he claims that Eve's attraction was too powerful, an accusation against God's creation, and further accuses Eve of causing his fall. Though rebuked by the Son, "Was shee thy God?" (10.145), Adam refuses any responsibility. Eve becomes, by contrast, the more heroic of the pair: "The serpent me beguil'd and I did eat" (10.162). The honesty she exhibits will lead them out of this hell.

Before that point, however, Adam passes through a complex psychological development, much like the stages of a person who learns he is dying. At first his guilt is unbearable, as the responsibility for destroying his progeny beings to dawn on him. In his anger he blames God for creating him and asks for death. The contract was too hard, and, moreover, he did not ask to be created. Adam is like Job. Both men challenge God and curse their creation. The parallel gives perspective on such outcries as these: "Did I request thee, Maker, from my Clay / To mould me Man" (10.743–44), and "Wherefore didst thou beget me? I sought it not" (10.762). Adam could well have exclaimed with Job: "Let the day perish wherein I was born, and the night in which it was said, There is a man child conceived" (Job 3:3).

But both finally come to accept life on God's terms; earlier they had accepted its joy, so now they must learn to accept its sorrow as well. Later it is revealed to both that God's ways are more complex than they can conceive and that His power is infinitely beyond their own. Life is a gift in the hands of God. They cannot cavil at the terms, since they have already implicitly accepted the contract. Adam reaches much the same conclusion even Satan arrived at earlier: "his doom is fair" (10.769). Both accept the justice of God's ways, though each must battle down pride first. But, unlike Adam, Satan cannot submit. Adam's lament, we see, is therapeutic in part. He hoped to find relief in complaint, a sour but consoling literary invention: "And in a troubl'd Sea of passion tost, / Thus to disburd'n sought with sad complaint" (10.718–19). The expression of his pain helps him accept his guilt. He begins to fear for his progeny should death not arrive. If he reasons the guilt of those who are his innocent descendants, he surmises that guilt is inborn and must be washed clean by a scapegoat but knows it is not to be himself. Though he wanders in intellectual "Mazes" (10.830), like the fallen angels (2.561), Adam takes the first step toward his own regeneration by accepting the guilt of his posterity himself. Why should the innocent suffer: "On mee, mee only, as the source and spring / Of all corruption, all the blame lights due; / So might the wrath" (10.832–34).

Now the echoes are not to Job or to Satan, but to the Son at His offer to die for man:

> Behold mee then, mee for him, life for life
> I offer, on mee let thine anger fall;
> Account mee man; I for his sake will leave
> Thy bosom, and this glory next to thee
> Freely put off, and for him lastly die.
> (3.236–40)

The Satanic contrast to these speeches is the adversary's assertion of the subjective-case *I*: "What matter where, if I be still the same, / And what I should be, all but less than hee / Whom Thunder hath made greater?" (1.256–58). Satan's egoistic assertiveness dwindles in comparison with the Christian heroism of sacrificing oneself for others. The new hero dies passively for his people as the older hero died fighting on the battlefield. But Adam is limited now after his fall: he cannot reach an end of his sufferings by ratiocination. He offers himself for his posterity, choosing to die and choosing not to produce a guilty race—"Why comes not Death?" (10.854)—but he can offer no other solution. Disillusioned of excuses, his burden of guilt crushes his will to live, as in Milton's second degree of death. Worse, he still holds Eve responsible: "Out of my sight, thou Serpent, that name best / Befits thee with him leagu'd" (10.867–68).

While Adam has accepted the condition of his suffering, he cannot fully accept the cause; his anger at Eve displaces his anger at himself. What remains of his superior intellect and what he receives of God's grace enable Adam to reconcile himself in part, but his resolution is insufficient without Eve. It is easier for Adam to feel sorrow for the unborn than to forgive Eve. Ironically, Adam wallows in a misogyny that smacks of the glibness of bumper-sticker morality:

> O why did God,
> Creator wise, that peopl'd highest Heav'n

Eden

With Spirits Masculine, create at last
This novelty on Earth, this fair defect
Of Nature, and not fill the World at once
With Men as Angels without Feminine,
Or find some other way to generate
Mankind? this mischief had not then befall'n,
And more that shall befall, innumerable
Disturbances on Earth through Female snares,
And strait conjunction with this Sex: for either
He never shall find out fit Mate, but such
As some misfortune brings him, or mistake,
Or whom he wishes most shall seldom gain
Through her perverseness, but shall see her gain'd
By a far worse, or if she love, withheld
By Parents, or his happiest choice too late
Shall meet, already linkt and Wedlock-bound
To a fell Adversary, his hate or shame:
Which infinite calamity shall cause
To Human life, and household peace confound.
(10.888–908)

Far from male chauvinism, Milton satirizes the misogynist as an angry fallen creature blaming his helpmeet for not being his mother in preventing the ills that he creates. In his deteriorated condition, Adam believes that the angels have a gender.

After the Fall and in a different sense than before it, man and woman are dependent upon each other or, by extension, upon society in general, since Adam and Eve are the world population at this moment in the poem. Before the Fall they were intellectual, sexual, and spiritual companions but had benefit of divine instruction at key moments. In the postlapsarian world, they are alone and mutually dependent; without Eve, Adam would nurse his misogyny alone, the rest of the human race would not be at all, and neither Adam nor Eve would find peace. Without Adam's help, Eve would resort to the absolute birth control and suicide she suggests. Yet the most heroic step is Eve's. Her action parallels that of the Son's sacrifice for man on the cross. Like the Son overhearing the Father's prophecy of the Fall of man, Eve is moved to pity at the sight of Adam's fall. Her speech, like Adam's earlier, echoes the Son's and Satan's repeated use of the first-person pronoun; this repetition is a kind of chant of determination in the soul. But whereas Satan's was egoistic and Adam's limited to his imagined progeny, Eve's is closest to the self-sacrifice of the Son. She undertakes what Adam could not: to request forgiveness. The climax of *Paradise Lost* is Eve's eating of the fruit, but not even tragedy ends on a totally hopeless note. In Milton's poem, a strong countermotion begins— man's regeneration—a process that will not be complete till the end of time, but which is prophesied in the significantly subordinate sentence at the beginning of the poem: "till one greater Man / Restore us, and regain the blissful Seat" (1.4–5). In her reply to Adam, Eve composes a new poem, one not needed in prelapsarian Eden, the carpe-diem poem, the argument that time is passing and that silly quarrels and quibbling scruples should be overlooked in a world of lost time and sure death. Eve accepts the termination of time now, while Adam expresses a wounded ego: the collapse of an idealist can be overwhelming. Ironically, Eve approaches Adam in spite of his rebuff and his antifeminist diatribe in order to win his favor through pity, love, logic, self-blame, and finally self-sacrifice:

> Forsake me not thus, *Adam,* witness Heav'n
> What love sincere, and reverence in my heart
> I bear thee, and unweeting have offended,
> Unhappily deceiv'd; thy suppliant
> I beg, and clasp thy knees; bereave me not,
> Whereon I live, thy gentle looks, thy aid,
> Thy counsel in this uttermost distress,
> My only strength and stay: forlorn of thee,
> Whither shall I betake me, where subsist?
> While yet we live, scarce one short hour perhaps,
> Between us two let there be peace, both joining,
> As join'd in injuries, one enmity
> Against a Foe by doom express assign'd us,
> That cruel Serpent: On mee exercise not
> Thy hatred for this misery befall'n,
> On me already lost, mee than thyself
> More miserable; both have sinn'd, but thou

> Against God only, I against God and thee,
> And to the place of judgment will return,
> There with my cries importune Heav'n, that all
> The sentence from thy head remov'd may light
> On me, sole cause to thee of all this woe,
> Mee mee only just object of his ire.
> (10.914–36)

There is a particular significance to the iconography of this scene. Eve kneels before Adam, begging forgiveness: "thy suppliant / I beg, and clasp thy knees" (10.917–18). This image is central to classical epic; the suppliant clasping the knees and being rebuffed is crucial to the tragedies included in classical epic poetry: the suppliants Chryses and Priam, at the beginning and at the end of the *Iliad,* Odysseus in disguise begging at his own door (*Odyssey,* 17), Turnus stretching his arm to Aeneas at the climax of the *Aeneid*—to name only a few of these key images. The epic suppliant is usually rejected and the punishment of the rejector follows, or is fated to follow, sometimes leaving its mark upon a whole later race. Zeus is the defender of the suppliant, and a whole morality in the heroic world of battle depends upon the role of mercy in society. That Christianity should raise up the suppliant, that a morality of forgiveness can replace a morality of revenge, is clearly Milton's point here. The new heroism is that of the Son and Eve, fulfilling what was prayed for in the heroic epics but seldom achieved.

In Milton, pity wins out over revenge, not because Adam realizes that his charges against Eve are false but because Eve takes guilt upon herself and offers herself to die for Adam, thereby disarming him. Arguing will never achieve what love will, in Milton's view. *Mea culpa,* the fault is mine, is good psychology *and* theology. Eve emphasizes *her* sin and *her* role in the Fall. Freed of accusation from without, Adam can now feel Eve's double anguish caused by betraying God's commandment and by tempting Adam to sin.

Adam responds by realizing how difficult it would be for Eve to bear the punishment alone. His pity in return completes the groundwork for regeneration. Finally he sees beyond his pain to hers. Adam realizes further that he is causing part of her suffering: "my displeasure bear'st [thou] so ill" (10.952). Reassured in love, Adam suggests cooperation and mutual love to ease the facts of fate. Adam now imagines that death is not imminent, but "a long day's dying to augment our pain" (10.964), a world of pain to follow. Eve's ability to deal with realistic aspects of their dilemma produces this alternative for the future: do not have children, do not pass on misery. Further, she asks if life is worth living in the face of possible suffering and inevitable death? And if Adam thinks abstinence too difficult, Eve suggests, now quite determined: "Let us seek Death, or he not found, supply / With our hands his Office ourselves" (10.1001–2). Their situation is analogous to the human condition in general, but they are facing it for the first time—the heroic acceptance of life's terms for everyone. All literature answers the question whether life is worth living in a positive way. Historically, *Paradise Lost* answers the question directly and first.

Adam reasons that they will not escape pain but that life is beneficent in spite of pain and death. He recalls that the Son pitied them as He judged them and that He judged without anger, that He clothed them, and that He gave them fire to warm them. He knows that life can be overloved, and so its end does not cancel its pleasure. That good will win out in the future Adam knows from the Son's promise that the serpent, principle of evil in the world, will lose to the seed of future generations: "Between Thee and the Woman I will put / Enmity, and between thine and her Seed; / Her Seed shall bruise thy head, thou bruise his heel" (10.179–81). Still to learn more of what death will be from Michael and mustering, unknown to them, resources with which to accept the expulsion from the Garden, Adam and Eve both become suppliants: "with tears / Watering the ground, and with thir sighs the Air / Frequenting, sent from hearts contrite, in sign / Of sorrow unfeign'd, and humiliation meek" (10.1101–04).

In book 3, the Father had prophesied that all would be given the chance of salvation. Proof of this comes for Adam and Eve in the form of "Prevenient Grace" (11.3), the grace that comes before repentance and softens hearts. Now they are free to accept or reject such divine mercy. Their acceptance enables them to utter prayers: "Inspir'd and wing'd for Heav'n with speedier flight / Than loudest Oratory" (11.7–8). They retain, then, some of their prelapsarian linguistic skills in the form of a true rhetoric of prayer to conquer the false rhetoric of Satan. Through new powers as a seer, Adam regains confidence in trusting the future. So far Adam and Eve have built upon the Son's prophecy of the seed of the woman bruising the head of the serpent but without knowing what that means. On the other hand, they have not learned of death in all its four stages either. For this knowledge, which is beyond their imaginations, must be presented by a higher power.

VIII

Michael's Vision: The Future as Prophecy

Like other epics, *Paradise Lost* extends its action and the significance of that action into the future, just as its geographical catalogs and historical allusions extend the poem in space. The historical ordering of events at the end of the poem puts these geographical and historical allusions into a system. Unlike other epics, *Paradise Lost* has the vision at the end of the epic for the extension into the future, into our own lives, as the Christian poet intends it. The events of the poem are now seen as a prologue to human history, a key to its interpretation. The biblical epic was a Renaissance genre in itself, whose model was Exodus 15, the "Mosaic Hymn," a summary of Hebrew history. From his Christian and linear view of history, Milton selects certain episodes to represent the course of events. These events are designed to teach Adam what he must know about the future in order to live in a fallen world, the same facts the reader must know, but the reader, of course, views them as history. Some readers have noted a falling off of Milton's aggressively personal style in the last two books of the poem. This was inevitable, for Milton here relies more on the language of the Bible, especially the King James Version, out of respect for which he relies upon its inspired words sometimes at the expense of his own. Milton's purpose is to lead the reader to the Bible. Moreover, Milton's audience was so well tuned to the Bible that the selection of scenes and the variations that Milton rings on them would be easily recognized.

From the wide and heterogeneous collection of literary types in the Bible, the poet selects only a few and for specific themes. Epic prophecies were usually gloomy portraits of foreign wars and civil wars determined by fate. Milton in contrast emphasizes the achievements of individuals, whose independence should inspire Adam to the tough individuality of a Puritan morality, the pattern established by Abdiel in the war in heaven.

Besides this thematic orientation, the reader finds another dramatic element in Adam's reactions to these events. Like the chorus in Greek tragedy, Adam comments upon, and reacts to, the scenes. Like Dante, Adam feels pity, outrage, lust, fear, sorrow, despair, shame, and joy at the pageant of history. But, unlike Dante, Adam is personally involved in the whole aftermath of the Fall because he is the cause of human history in its fallen form. Michael's counterreactions help Adam assimilate and accept the new facts of death, guilt, suffering, and triumph in this our life. Adam regains some of the composure lost at the Fall: the only balm for present evil is future hope.

It is appropriate that Michael, "like to God," presents the vision. He represents the warrior angel who appears in art dressed in battle regalia and who will battle the Dragon of Revelation at the end of time; he points to the postlapsarian history of the world and to the need for Christians to struggle against evil. He does not represent pure militarism but spiritual warfare. He solaces Adam with the perspective of eternity, soothing the expulsion from the Garden with the promise of redemption, the vision, and moral advice. Michael alters Adam and Eve's view of the world from that of being changeless in a changeless place to that of fallen humanity living with change, a sort of leaving off of the stable world of childhood. Eve, who takes most to heart the leaving of her "children," the flowers she has tended and has grown close to, is told:

> Lament not *Eve*, but patiently resign
> What justly thou hast lost; nor set thy heart,

> Thus over-fond, on that which is not thine;
> Thy going is not lonely, with thee goes
> Thy Husband, him to follow thou art bound;
> Where he abides, think there thy native soil.
> (11.287–92)

Death and change are the price of life: man must learn to give up. His consolation is that all share the same world. Adam commends the gentleness that Michael shows in dealing with the expelled, the dying.

Only the future can console Adam and Eve, so Michael reveals it as worth living, though full of "supernal Grace contending / With sinfulness of Men" (11.359–60). Michael not only reveals history as the Bible presents it, but shows how to interpret history, advocating the use of the mind in abstracting sustenance—hope and wisdom—from inert fact. So the reader learns that God's ways are just and Adam learns what the consequences of his sin are and what mercy God will show his descendants. But extracting themes is not enough: the truths of history must be applied, as well as identified. Michael shares the vision with Adam:

> thereby to learn
> True patience, and to temper joy with fear
> And pious sorrow, equally inur'd
> By moderation either state to bear,
> Prosperous or adverse: so shalt thou lead
> Safest thy life, and best prepar'd endure
> Thy mortal passage when it comes.
> (11.360–66)

Since Adam's powers are now diminished, Michael must spell out what Adam might once have extracted himself—reader-response is a fallen school of criticism. Adam must relearn the lesson of moderation violated by the eating of the fruit. Michael's Aristotelianism extends even to moderation in the love of life itself, for death and pain are now part of the fabric of things.

Michael's Vision

A rough outline of the events of Michael's vision are:

1. Cain and Abel
2. A Lazar House (Hospital)
3. The Tent Dwellers
4. Towns at War
5. Noah
6. Nimrod and the Tower of Babel
7. Abraham and his Generations:
    A. Plagues of Egypt
    B. Moses
    C. The Nativity
    D. Crucifixion
    E. Redemption.

Within these scenes, we find varying degrees of joy and sorrow that Adam must verify and accept.

From the Cain and Abel incident, Adam learns of one type of death: that caused by jealousy and fratricide. Through pity and remorse, Adam experiences death for the first time. Surprisingly, Michael warns him not to grieve to excess and to keep death in perspective, for the crime will be avenged: "and th' other's Faith approv'd / Lose no reward, though here thou see him die, / Rolling in dust and gore" (11.458–60).

The Lazar House episode extends Adam's conception of death to more lingering and, for that, more painful, forms. At the sight of mental and bodily disease, Adam questions whether life is worth the risk at all: "Better end here unborn" (11.502), a thought reminiscent of Eve's proposals about suicide and birth control. Adam still thinks of suffering as unnatural, since he was created in the image of God. He learns from Michael not only that it is naturalized now, but that suffering can be the result of man's own excesses, which moderation can alleviate. Michael's application of the theory of the Golden Mean extends to the familiar image of the root once more. Death is now natural; man is another plant in the garden who at best may live:

> till like ripe Fruit thou drop
> Into thy Mother's lap, or be with ease
> Gather'd, not harshly pluckt, for death mature:
> This is old age; but then thou must outlive
> Thy youth, thy strength, thy beauty, which will change
> To wither'd weak and gray; thy Senses then
> Obtuse, all taste of pleasure must forgo,
> To what thou hast, and for the Air of youth
> Hopeful and cheerful, in thy blood will reign
> A melancholy damp of cold and dry
> To weigh thy Spirits down, and last consume
> The Balm of Life.
> (11.535–46)

Such are not words of consolation, but they are meant to make Adam face the future. He counters with Eve's notion that perhaps suicide is best, confusing life's dismal ending with all its benefits received till that point. Michael reiterates his point that death is the price of life and that loving life over-much to the point of not accepting death is a vice: "Nor love thy Life nor hate: but what thou liv'st / Live well, how long or short permit to Heav'n" (11.553–54).

The third scene, the plain, gives Adam some pleasures and accomplishments to anticipate, at least for his offspring: music, in which he catches a glimpse of the harp and organ and hears snatches of a fugue, as well as metal work, the casting of tools and other objects. One promises pleasure, the other promises ease in labor: in short, civilization. Because not all pleasures are fruitful, Michael shows Adam a bevy of beautiful women, suggesting not that woman is more corrupt than man but that Adam must become aware of his major weakness and be cured of his misogyny. At first, Adam is struck with admiration and possible pleasure, but the women, descendants of Cain, seduce the men who forget to thank God, Who gave them their skills. Pleasure has led to egotism. Michael tells, but does not show, that these couples will cause destruction in the world, since their only principle is their own pleasure. He thereby urges Adam to weigh the outcome of pleasure and not just its appearance and promise. Characteristically, Adam blames the women, as he had earlier blamed Eve: "But still I see the tenor of Man's woe / Holds on the same, from Woman to begin" (11.632–33).

The antifeminist and false etymology of *woman* from "woe of man" was a commonplace (the word derives from the Anglo-Saxon *wifeman*, "man" being originally applied to both genders). The false etymology, employed even in the commentaries to Genesis, is subverted by Michael: "From Man's effeminate slackness it begins / Said th' Angel, who should better hold his place / By wisdom, and superior gifts receiv'd" (11.634–36).

The fourth scene shows political death: towns at war. This inset parallels the Shield of Achilles in *Iliad* 18. With that and other classical allusions, Milton invokes the world of classical heroism he has been revaluating throughout the poem and which followed shortly after the events in Eden in the Renaissance calendar of history. In this vision of war, siege, and pillage, mass slaughter is a result of those marriages shown before. Yet to leaven the bitterness, Michael introduces the one-good-man theme (here Enoch), which keeps ideals alive in a dark time. Though heaven saves Enoch, Adam is shocked and saddened. Michael explains that the old heroic code of warfare is a means of gaining fame and offers a kind of immortality, but he denounces the code and helps us see Milton's conception of heroism:

> For in those days Might only shall be admir'd,
> And Valor and Heroic Virtue call'd;
> To overcome in Battle, and subdue
> Nations, and bring home spoils with infinite
> Man-slaughter, shall be held the highest pitch
> Of human Glory, and for Glory done
> Of triumph, to be styl'd great Conquerors,
> Patrons of Mankind, Gods, and Sons of Gods,
> Destroyers rightlier call'd and Plagues of men.
> Thus Fame shall be achiev'd, renown on Earth,

And what most merits fame in silence hid.
(11.689–99)

Michael juxtaposes the righteous Enoch, "the only righteous in a
World perverse" (11.701), to all the heroes of classical epic. True heroism consists in doing right.

The fifth scene shows what destruction results from lechery and
riot and what reward the good shall discover. Adam grieves over those
lost in adultery, prostitution, rape, and brawls. The scene shows that
vice exists in times of peace as well as in times of war. Adam is by
now so paralyzed with grief and fainting that he wishes not to know
any more of the future, but Michael always shows a reason to live in
spite of pain. Adam anticipates Noah and his family destroyed by fa-
mine and anguish; Eden, too, is flooded, so that Adam will realize that
God is not limited to any one place and can be found everywhere.
Adam rejoices at seeing another good man saved in the promise of the
rainbow to Noah, a promise of a covenant between man and God,
Who promises never to destroy the world again through water (the
rainbow in ancient times was a sign that the gods had ceased to war
with man and had hung their weapon in the sky to symbolize peace).
Fire will come next, but it will "purge all things new" (11.900): "Such
grace shall one just Man find in his sight" (11.890).

Michael's vision now becomes more spiritualized: Adam, tired
with sights must not see but hear about "Man as from a second stock
proceed" (12.7). Such perception is more fitting for man's future state
of interpreting biblical texts. Adam now hears his sin of rebellion repeated, as he saw his sin of sensuality (uxoriousness) repeated in the
first half of the vision. Such rebellion is in the will and is better com-
prehended by the ear and one's own imagination. The rebel is the evil
counterpart of the one good man and the human equivalent of Satan.
Adam comprehends the wrong in Nimrod's aspirations to power and
reasons against absolute rulers on earth and for equality among men,
points commonly made in Milton's political tracts. Nimrod's attempt
to topple God by means of the Tower of Babel helps Adam to understand Satan and Eve's impulses at the Fall. Human history becomes a

textbook of good and evil motives. Often Adam reacts with horror and anger, which Michael approves, explaining that liberty is lost, so reason loses sway and passions rule, an unfolding in history of Adam's own psychological state immediately after the Fall.

In Michael's reading of history, man's disobedience and neglect of right reason (conscience and reason) leads to the selection of a chosen race, the Jews, represented by another solitary hero, Abraham. Through Abraham's race, mankind is blessed. God demands that man worship Him, not his own acts. He demands humility. Like individuals, tribes must learn governance before they can be rewarded with the Land of Canaan. Through this very biblical section of the poem, Milton relies upon typological interpretations from the Old Testament (i.e., Old Testament symbolical foreshadowings of the New Testament); thus the wandering in the desert can be seen in Christian terms as man lost in the wilderness of sin till one greater man arrive, Christ, of whom Moses was a "type." The Hebrew Law is imposed to control chaos in society, but is interpreted as a stop-gap measure along the way to a mediator between man and God. In this manner, Michael, closely following St. Paul's explanation of the Old Testament, interprets the prophecy given to Adam concerning the bruising of the serpent's head to mean the coming of the Son in the form of Christ. History as a series of tableaux yields to history as summary. Michael deliberately avoids relating the military history of the Jews; their history is summed up in the miracle of the sun standing still in Gibeon. What is more important is the Pauline doctrine that the Law showed forth man's sinful nature, in other words, guilt. Such a feeling was not removed by animal sacrifices, rites, or observance of the Law, so a greater cleansing force was needed: "From shadowy Types to Truth, from Flesh to Spirit, / From imposition of strict Laws, to free / Acceptance" (12.303–05).

Sin and corruption lead to being conquered. Because Solomon was earthly and corrupt, the need arose for a heavenly deliverer from the Babylonian captivity of the Hebrews. According to Michael's reading of history, Israel lost its independence to enable Christ to be born barred, symbolically and actually, from his birth right.

When Adam learns of the Son's sacrifice, he realizes that good will proceeds from his sin as well as pain and death. He makes a new covenant with life, accepting it as a mixture of good and evil. Michael's vision becomes more of a dialogue toward the end, as Adam's insight, like the blind narrator's, begins to dawn inwardly from what he hears. His sight has been cleared, as was promised, with euphrasy (joy) and rue (sorrow) (11.414). But he is still motivated by a desire for revenge against Satan: where and when will Satan receive his bruise?

Michael again lifts Adam to heights of symbolic interpretations by explaining to Adam the Theory of Accommodation: the wounds will not be "local wounds" (12.387). Like Paradise, Satan is a state of mind, so the adversary himself will not be destroyed but rather his works in man. In this fashion, Adam learns the ultimate truth of history: goodness will win out: the "Law of Faith / Working through love" (12.488–89), "O goodness infinite, goodness immense! / That all this good of evil shall produce" (12.469–70). The difficulty of that task is reflected in the tortuous syntax of the last line. Adam begins to be a prophet, too, emulating Michael. He speculates correctly concerning the future followers of Christ, showing his renewed abilities:

> But say, if our deliverer up to Heav'n
> Must reascend, what will betide the few
> His faithful, left among th' unfaithful herd,
> The enemies of truth; who then shall guide
> His people, who defend? will they not deal
> Worse with his followers than with him they dealt?
> (12.479–84)

Faith replaced the Law, but corruption of the clergy will follow and laws shall try to force conscience and fail. Adam learns to keep an external perspective on all of history, to focus on the sureness of redemption, not on the vicissitudes of political events, "Till time stand fixt: beyond is all abyss, / Eternity, whose end no eye can reach" (12.555–56). Again like Job, Adam learns that the awesome power of God extends beyond his comprehension, forcing his submission.

Michael's Vision

Michael proclaims him to have manifested a saving faith, but such faith cannot be void of works. In order to apply his knowledge of faith and love, Adam requires the classical virtues of patience and temperance. But Michael does not present these ideas in an abstract void: they are the result of what Adam has witnessed on the mount in paradise. Having learned to interpret life symbolically and having been corrected in a series of errors, Adam descends from the top of speculation to the lowly plain of living and working. Michael then escorts Adam and Eve, their hands in his hand, a picture of launching children into the world ("education") and leaves them in each other's hands, which separated at the Fall (9.385–86), in order to rely on that society that saved them from suicide and genocide. Mindful of the Fall, but trusting to a better future, they assume our lives, an unsure journey with euphrasy and rue:

> The World was all before them, where to choose
> Thir place of rest, and Providence thir guide:
> They hand in hand with wand'ring steps and slow,
> Through *Eden* took their solitary way.
> (12.646–49)

IX

The Narrator:
Evil Days and Evil Tongues

Adam's descent to the level of fallen human experience brings him closer not only to the reader's experience of life, but even more immediately to the experience of the narrator. Adam's reception of his insightful vision is exactly what the narrator prays for. The narrator describes the event:

> *Michael* from *Adam's* eyes the Film remov'd
> Which that false Fruit that promis'd clearer sight
> Had bred; then purg'd with Euphrasy and Rue
> The visual Nerve, for he had much to see;
> And from the Well of Life three drops instill'd.
> So deep the power of these Ingredients pierc'd,
> Ev'n to the inmost seat of mental sight.
> (11.412–18)

Adam receives the antidote to the "drop serene" (3.25) that quenched the narrator's sight and receives what the narrator requested:

> So much the rather thou Celestial Light
> Shine inward, and the mind through all her powers

The Narrator

Irradiate, there plant eyes, all mist from thence
Purge and disperse, that I may see and tell
Of things invisible to mortal sight.
(3.51–55)

The narrator receives his wish by being inspired to sing of spiritual events and by having the help of two celestial narrators, Raphael and Michael, who inform the narrator as well as being his characters. Michael's revelation to Adam is the most authentic answer to the narrator's request for illumination, because Michael reveals the Bible itself. Hence all men will have the possibility of visions. Moreover, Michael's vision is a comfort to the narrator, for he has suffered firsthand from Satan's rebellion and Adam's sin, being blind in a hostile world.

The narrator in *Paradise Lost* is one of Milton's most original contributions to the epic genre. Epic narrators up till Milton had revealed little about themselves. So little was known about Homer that seven cities could claim to be his birthplace. The tradition was maintained, more or less, until Dante used himself as a character in his epicizing of the medieval dream vision, where the dreamer could have a major role. But in both the *Divine Comedy* and the dream visions, the narrator functions on a level with the characters: he is part of the dream. Milton could not enter into paradise or heaven, as Dante could be led through hell, purgatory, and heaven, without clumsy self-aggrandizing. Milton presents himself as the poet, not constructing, but inspired to sing by the Holy Spirit, the power of God that inspired Moses and other biblical writers. In the Renaissance, more use of autobiography appeared: Ariosto, Spenser, and DuBartas could incorporate biographical data about themselves or their patrons into their epics. But Milton's narrator plays a more complex role in his epic. In general, he is a poet, prophet, scholar, fallen man; in particular, he is John Milton himself: blind and maligned in the post-Restoration world of England. Milton is one of the earliest writers in crisis. His personal relationship with his characters and his self-revelation is in keeping with his conception of poetry as a personal art, wherein the poet can reveal himself more appropriately than in prose, as he states in his *Reason of Church Government* (Prose, 1:808). But Milton presents himself simultaneously with generalized man. His life has interest because we want to participate in the depth of the writer's feeling and experience, which at times is beyond our own.

In order to participate more fully with Milton's narrator, we must see him in context. First, he reveals the interest of his age in the Divine Poetry Movement. When Milton was three years old and probably already thinking about being a poet, a religious revival was sweeping London. Witty Jack Donne had already taken religious orders. In the many churches that filled London and in Milton's own Bread Street, Richard Stock harangued boys and girls for not knowing their bibles. Preachers were so popular that a congregation gathered at five A.M. to hear the epistles of Saint Paul expounded. In poetry, the movement advocated religious experience as basic and all other poetry as insufficient metaphor for true experience, which was spiritual. Earlier Renaissance poetry was decried as a trivial pursuit of an earthly goal: the mistress or lover, sexual or profane love. Now the subjective imagination was tapped through meditation and vision. The question was what spiritual route to follow; the Reformation made religion a dangerous and intellectually stimulating topic. Political control was still in the hands of a conservative church with the power of life and death. The printing press and the proliferation of books and pamphlets allowed ideas to circulate and sects to form and dissolve rapidly. At the root of the controversy lay key questions of morality, freedom, education, and political power.

Second, the narrator is that scholarly boy who studied his classics at home and at school and then at home again. Milton was a financially independent, privately tutored child who cultivated music and poetry, cut off from the crime and poverty of London. In this context, the narrator is the inheritor of the literary traditions, classical, biblical, continental, and English, the descendent of Homer, Virgil, Moses, Tasso, Spenser, and others. Both poet and critic. The world of books, where you are what you read.

Third, we find the disillusioned revolutionary: the defender of the regicide, blind and once imprisoned and sentenced to death, after a generation of Civil War politics that came to nothing at the time, though the power of the bishops had been broken and the cycle of democratic revolutions begun. Politics seems irredeemable to this part of the narrational voice. Now he makes a revolution of his own, a literary one.

As a result of these three aspects, the narrator can hardly be neutral. Nor is neutrality always a good literary strategy. The narrator adds a dramatic dimension to the poem, a center whose experience radiates throughout history, throughout his own life and times, and throughout ours. Moreover, he is inspired by God. Milton's narrator gives his poem dramatic tension, depth, complexity, and authority.

The combination of inspiration and the learning that the narrator has displayed in training to be a poet reflects Milton's poetics. He combines the Greek concepts of *poiesis,* poetry as made by a skilled craftsman, and poetry as inspired by the muse, Homer's *aoidê.* As a prophet-poet, he is inspired by God, but as a scholar-poet he has trained himself to be the fit vessel. As prophet, the bard knows what to say; as craftsman he makes the forms to express it in.

In his *Reason of Church Government,* Milton pictures the poet as an inspired Old Testament prophet, "soaring in the high region of his fancies with his garland and singing robes about him" (Prose, 1:808). In *Of Education,* he tells us that poetry is "more simple, sensuous and passionate" (Prose, 2:403) than rhetoric. In "Ad Patrem," the poem to his father, Milton emphasizes the sacred nature of the bard. Translated from the Latin by Merritt Y. Hughes, it reads: "You should not despise the poet's task, divine song, which preserves some spark of Promethean fire and is the unrivalled glory of the heaven-born human mind and an evidence of our ethereal origin and celestial descent" (17–20). Yet, "these abilities, wheresoever they be found, are the inspired gift of God rarely bestow'd" (Prose, 1:816). They are given by "that eternall Spirit who can enrich with all utterance and knowledge, and sends out his Seraphim with the hallow'd fire of his Altar to touch and purify the lips of whom he pleases" (Prose, 1:820–21), imitating the call of Isaiah (6). Such was Milton's passion for fame, justly earned. If many would, today, substitute *the unconscious* for Milton's metaphor of the promptings of God, little else has changed. This side of Milton must have appealed to William Blake.

But Milton immediately adds the artisan to the prophet: "to this must be added industrious and select reading, steddy observation, insight into all seemly and generous arts and affaires" (Prose, 1:821). For his part, Milton dedicates himself to "labour and intent study (which I take to be my portion in this life)" (Prose, 1:810), whom "none hath by more studious ways endeavour'd, and with more unwearied spirit that none shall, that I dare almost averre of myself, as farre as life and free leasure will extend" (Prose, 1.820). Later, he confesses to wearing out "almost a whole youth" in study (Prose, 1:869). The program of reading alluded to by Milton includes all the literature available to him, a "ceaselesse round of study and reading" (Prose, 1:891). In *Of Education,* Milton advocates reading critics to ballast literature with theory: "which in *Aristotles poetics,* in *Horace,* and the *Italian* commentaries of *Castelvetro, Tasso, Mazzoni,* and others, teaches what the laws are of a true *Epic* poem, what of a *Dramatic,* what of a *Lyric*" (Prose, 2:404–5). This reading should lead to conscious imitation: ". . . whether that Epick form whereof the two poems of *Homer,* and those other two of *Virgil* and *Tasso* are a diffuse, and the book of *Job* a brief model: or whether the rules of *Aristotle* herein are strictly to be kept, or nature to be follow'd." (Prose, 1:813). Milton continues after this passage to list and explicate models for the writer. By the time he wrote *Paradise Lost* over twenty years later, imitation of models had led to emulation, so the bard in the poem can claim that his "avent'rous Song" "with no middle flight intends to soar / Above th' *Aonian* Mount" (1.13–15), Mount Helicon sacred to the classical poets. In book 9 he sweeps aside other epics and romances, because his poem is the portrait of true heroism. In this passage we find blended the poet of "unpremeditated Verse" (9.24) and the scholar-poet who rose each day at 4 A.M., even in blindness, to study the Hebrew Bible:

> Sad task, yet argument
> Not less but more Heroic than the wrath

Of stern *Achilles* on his Foe pursu'd
Thrice Fugitive about *Troy* Wall; or rage
Of *Turnus* for *Lavinia* disespous'd,
Or *Neptune's* ire or *Juno's,* that so long
Perplex'd the *Greek* and *Cytherea's* Son;
If answerable style I can obtain
Of my Celestial Patroness, who deigns
Her nightly visitation unimplor'd,
And dictates to me slumb'ring, or inspires
Easy my unpremeditated Verse:
Since first this Subject for Heroic Song
Pleas'd me long choosing, and beginning late;
Not sedulous by Nature to indite
Wars, hitherto the only Argument
Heroic deem'd, chief maistry to dissect
With long and tedious havoc fabl'd Knights
In Battles feign'd; the better fortitude
Of Patience and Heroic Martyrdom
Unsung; or to describe Races and Games,
Or tilting Furniture, emblazon'd Shields,
Impreses quaint, Caparisons and Steeds;
Bases and tinsel Trappings, gorgeous Knights
At Joust and Tournament; then marshall'd Feast
Serv'd up in Hall with Sewers and Seneschals;
The skill of Artifice or Office mean,
Not that which justly gives Heroic name
To Person or to Poem. Mee of these
Nor skill'd nor studious, higher Argument
Remains, sufficient of itself to raise
That name, unless an age too late, or cold
Climate, or Years damp my intended wing
Deprest; and much they may, if all be mine,
Not Hers who brings it nightly to my Ear.
(9.13–47)

These lines obliquely contain Milton's method in *Paradise Lost,* and elsewhere: the mastering of the genre in which he writes, and then a revaluation and transformation of that genre into something new. Milton ended the epic in the old heroic sense and turned heroic poetry into a psychological drama of such stylistic force that it has been said that only the novel could continue where Milton stopped. Yet the poem remains unique.

Behind these lines also lies Milton's concept of the poet as specially chosen, an ideal artist with a special calling. In Elegy VI, he had distinguished between two types of poet, the trivial amorist and the serious epic poet:

> For many of the gods patronize the gay elegy and she calls whom she will to her measures. Liber and Erato, Ceres and Venus are at hand to help her, and beside his rosy mother is the stripling Cupid. For such poets, then, grand banquets are allowable and frequent potations of old wine. But he whose theme is wars and heaven under Jupiter in his prime, and pious heroes and chieftains half-divine, and he who sings now of the sacred counsels of the gods on high, and now of the infernal realms, where the fierce dog howls, let him live sparingly like the Samian teacher [Pythagoras]; and let herbs furnish his innocent diet. Let the purest water stand beside him in a bowl of beech and let him drink sober draughts from the pure spring. Beyond this, his youth must be innocent of crime and chaste, his conduct irreproachable and his hands stainless. His character should be like yours, O Priest, when, glorious with sacred vestments and lustral water, you arise to go into the presence of the angry deities. (49–66; translation of Merritt Y. Hughes)

In his *Reason of Church Government,* Milton reiterates and elaborates on the special calling of the serious poet, whose pure poetry should emanate from his pure life. Not only does Milton idealize the poem, but also the poet. After emphasizing that the poet must always be critical in his reading, extracting what is best from other writers, he adds: "he who would not be frustrate of his hope to write well hereafter in laudable things, ought himselfe to bee a true Poem, that is, a composition, and patterne of the best and honourablest things; not presuming to sing high praises of heroick men, or famous Cities, unlesse he have in himself the experience and the practice of all that which is praise-worthy" (Prose, 1:890). Moral integrity, then, helps produce art. This same integrity is behind the narrator's stance as an example of the one good man living in evil times, like Abdiel, Moses,

Noah, and others in his text. Note that although the failure of the revolution stands behind the following lines biographically, they are hardly necessary to the generalized context:

> More safe I Sing with mortal voice unchang'd
> To hoarse or mute, though fall'n on evil days,
> On evil days though fall'n, and evil tongues;
> In darkness, and with dangers compast round,
> And solitude.
> (7.24–28)

More than just a confessional poet, Milton's bard reveals fallen man. His poetry is, like all epic poetry, public poetry, expressing the soul of his people, here expanded by Milton to the whole human race through the metaphor of Christianity. Behind this picture of humanity is the primal loneliness of all human existence. For Milton, poetry shows a way out, but through metaphor. Earlier I noted Milton's conception of the truth of the Bible being metaphorical through the Theory of Accommodation. Poetry, too, is metaphorical because it makes truth palatable: ". . . to those especially of soft and delicious temper who will not so much look upon Truth herselfe, unlesse they see her elegantly drest, that whereas the paths of honesty and good life appear now rugged and difficult, though they be indeed easy and pleasant, they would then appear to all men both easy and pleasant though they were rugged and difficult indeed" (Prose, 1:817–18). Poetry, for Milton, is a civilizer and vital to society.

X

Style and Versification: The Grand Masterpiece to Observe

The narrator receives from his "Celestial Patroness" (9.21) not only truth but form. Because he wrote of high "Things unattempted yet in Prose or Rhyme" (1.16), Milton wished the style of *Paradise Lost* to be: "my advent'rous Song, / That with no middle flight intends to soar / Above th' *Aonian Mount* (1.13–15). The narrator prays for the spirit that inspired Moses to write Genesis, though his poem will be an unsurpassed epic treatment of the theme of the Fall and of the promise of redemption. Milton left the paths of common speech to forge the highest medium of elevated language. Borrowing from Hebrew, Greek, Latin, and lesser-known English vocabularies and syntax, and borrowing also from Elizabethan drama, Milton deliberately created a tongue fit for God, angels, and prelapsarian man and woman. In order to judge Milton's style, we must place it in the context of a poem where all the characters by definition and the narrator by inspiration of the Holy Spirit speak a language beyond us mortals. Just as Michelangelo and other Renaissance artists gave such characters heroic bodies, Milton gave them heroic language. The characteristics that contribute to Milton's style are found in other writers as well, but certain characteristics common in *Paradise Lost* turn up rarely in other writers. Milton claims the right to use unusual terms of speech because his subject matter allows him, the principle he calls *decorum*. In listing separately the various aspects of Milton's style, I distort the natural sweep of the verse that he claimed was brought by the nocturnal muse. Yet Milton's achievement is very much a triumph of style, one that is worth analysis, not only because it reveals a mainstay of his poetry but simply because it often confuses the unwary reader. Much has been said about Milton's style and its marked difference from speech, both pro and con, but we must remember the great difficulties that Milton surmounted in attempting to create the sublime style in English almost single-handed. Thereby, he fulfilled his promise to do for his country what Greek, Latin, and Italian writers had done for theirs: create a divine language.

In order to create an elevated language, a poet must turn to the unusual, everything that deviates from normal speech, as Aristotle recommends in the *Poetics* (1458). The Renaissance epic poet wished to produce wonder in the reader; and wonder is not produced by a low or middle vocabulary. The very nature of epic, never mind divine epic, required elevation of diction and syntax. The danger is bombast. A poet can not elevate his language above what is fitting for his story without becoming humorous. We may analyze Milton's style simply by listing the ways in which he deviates from normal speech in order to strike the reader into admiration, not for the style alone, but for the divine story. Ultimately, God wrote *Paradise Lost*.

The first seven characteristics listed below are based upon James Holly Hanford's modifications of Raymond Dexter Havens's classifications; [25] the final seven are my own. This list is not to suggest that Milton's style is static; it is infinitely variable, constantly shifting (most drastically after the Fall), and rarely predictable. All these variations make the reader pause, think, and so become more engaged with the poem:

1. Inversion of the natural order of words and phrases:

> Them thus imploy'd beheld
> With pity Heav'ns high King. (5.219–20)

2. Ellipsis, the omission of words not necessary to the sense:

> (For Eloquence the Soul, Song charms the Sense.)
> (2.556)

3. Parentheses and Apposition (interrupted sense). Note here the syntax imitating the meaning:

> Thir song was Partial, but the harmony
> (What could it less when Spirits immortal sing?)
> Suspended Hell. (2.552–54)

4. The use of one part of speech for another: "grinn'd horrible" (2.846); "over the vast abrupt" (2.409).

5. Archaisms: *arede* (advise) (4.962), *attrite* (worn down by friction) (10.1073), *buxom* (obedient) (2.842), *emprise* (martial prowess) (11.642), *Frore* (cold) (2.595), *nocent* (harmful) (9.186).

6. Catalogs of exotic proper names, which George Saintsbury thought "intoxicating":[26]

> from the destin'd Walls
> Of *Cambalu*, seat of *Cathaian Can*,
> And *Samarchand* by *Oxus, Temir's* Throne,
> To *Paquin* of *Sinaean* Kings, and thence
> To *Agra* and *Lahore* of great *Mogul*
> . . .
> (11.387–411)

7. Unusual compound epithets, analogous to those in Homer: "night-warbling Bird" (5.40); "double-founted stream" (12.144); "Heav'n-warring Champions" (2.424).

8. Elevated diction: "Empyreal" (1.117); "Morn" (morning) (1.742); "Champaign" (open, flat country) (6.2).

9. Repetitions: phrases, words, words in different forms (polyptoton), syllables, letters:

> So Man, as is most just,
> Shall satisfy for Man, be judg'd and die,
> And dying rise, and raising with him raise
> His Brethren, ransom'd with his own dear life.
> So Heav'nly love shall outdo Hellish hate,
> Giving to death, and dying to redeem,
> So dearly to redeem what Hellish hate
> So easily destroy'd, and still destroys
> In those who, when they may, accept not grace.
> (3.294–302)

10. Allusions that invoke a specific earlier text, which Milton is "revising." In Revelation, John signals the defeat of the Dragon at the end of time with: "Therefore rejoice, ye heavens, and ye that dwell in them. Woe to the inhabiters of the earth and of the sea! for the devil is come down unto you, having great wrath, because he knoweth that he hath but a short time" (12:12). The narrator of *Paradise Lost* laments that the warning voice had not been there in the beginning to ward off the Fall from which the narrator suffers. At Satan's entrance into Eden, he exclaims:

> O for that warning voice, which he who saw
> Th' *Apocalypse,* heard cry in Heav'n aloud,
> Then when the Dragon put to second rout,
> Came furious down to be reveng'd on men,
> *Woe to the Inhabitants on Earth!* that now
> While time was, our first Parents had been warn'd
> The coming of thir secret foe.
> (4.1–7)

Milton's allusions are usually less direct, but often reward comparison with the parent text.

11. The use of the verse paragraph as the unit of composition.

12. Puns upon Greek, Latin, and Hebrew roots and meanings of words: "serpent error wand'ring" (7.302) suggests, respectively, the Greek and Latin "creep," the Latin "wander," and the Anglo-Saxon and Germanic equivalent in English. The Spirit of God's creation that "Dove-like satst brooding on the vast Abyss" (1.21) is literally doing what the Hebrew verb *rahaf*, used in Genesis (1, 2), means.

13. Contre-rejet: a surprising shift at the beginning of a line following a run-on line:

> thus they relate,
> Erring.
> (1.746–47)

> (For I glory in the name,
> Antagonist of Heav'n's Almighty King).
> (10.386–87)

14. Similes: extended similes as in all epics but sometimes in a series of two and sometimes open-ended, implying the inexpressible grandeur of the subject:

> He scarce had ceas't when the superior Fiend
> Was moving toward the shore; his ponderous shield
> Ethereal temper, massy, large and round,
> Behind him cast; the broad circumference
> Hung on his shoulders like the Moon, whose Orb
> Through Optic Glass the *Tuscan* Artist views
> At Ev'ning from the top of *Fesole,*
> Or in *Valdarno,* to descry new Lands,
> Rivers or Mountains in her spotty Globe.
> His Spear, to equal which the tallest Pine
> Hewn on *Norwegian* hills, to be the Mast
> Of some great Ammiral, were but a wand.
> (1.283–94)

Milton's similes have complex functions. For example, they often forecast the fallen world that the very event related has in some way caused. Thus, Satan's entrance into Eden causes both the animals to prey upon one another and the burglar to break into your room:

> At one slight bound high overleap'd all bound
> Of Hill or highest Wall, and sheer within
> Lights on his feet. As when a prowling Wolf,
> Whom hunger drives to seek new haunt for prey,
> Watching where Shepherds pen thir flocks at eve
> In hurdl'd Cotes amid the field secure,
> Leaps o'er the fence with ease into the Fold;
> Or as a Thief bent to unhoard the cash
> Of some rich Burger, whose substantial doors,
> Cross-barr'd and bolted fast, fear no assault,
> In at the window climbs, or o'er the tiles:
> So clomb this first grand Thief into God's Fold.
> (4.181–92)

Milton's style consists of more than merely varying and combining these elements. His Grand Style is an outgrowth of his subject and without his sense of decorum and his philosophical depth would degenerate into bombast.

VERSIFICATION

In *Paradise Lost,* Milton used blank verse, that is, a ten syllable line in which every other syllable receives an accent (iambic verse: ˘-). The verse is "blank" because it is unrhymed, which sounded strange at the time, for most English verse since Chaucer had rhymed. Milton defends his avoidance of rhyme in his note on "The Verse," which appears at the beginning of his poem. Blank verse is the equivalent in English of the Greek and Latin dactylic hexameter. Its length and its history still give it heroic associations. It is the vehicle for Shakespeare's plays, whose use combined with Milton's made it the basis for high English poetry thereafter:

> Ĭnvōke thy aīd tŏ my̆ advēnt'roŭs Sōng

Milton is very strict, allowing few variations in the iambic foot. The commonest shift is the first foot, which can become a trochee (an accented syllable followed by an unaccented syllable, the iamb reversed):

> Fāst bў tĥe Ōrăclē ŏf Gōd; Ĭ theñce
>
> (1.12)

In order to give his verse further variety, Milton varies the place where the major pause (caesura) in each line occurs. Usually the sense runs over the end of one line into another, drawing the reader through many lines, till punctuation gives relief, as Milton described in *L'Allegro*:

> with many a winding bout
> Of linked sweetness long drawn out,
> With wanton heed, and giddy cunning,
> The melting voice through mazes running;
> Untwisting all the chains that tie
> The hidden soul of harmony.
> (139–44)

Milton seems to have considered the verse paragraph as his unit of construction. The syntactical sense drives on, while the ten-syllable line acts as a counterweight, sometimes retarding, sometimes speeding the line. These counter forces produce tension and strength. Another characteristic of Milton's verse is the weighting of the unaccented syllable so that the movement of the verse is closer to a stately spondaic verse (two accented syllables in a row).

> Ŏf Mañ's Fīrst Dĭsŏbeđieñce, anđ tĥe Fruīt
> Ŏf thāt Fŏrbĭddeñ Trēe, whŏse mōrtăl taste
> Broūght Deāth iñtō thĕ Wo̅rld, añd aĺl ŏŭr wōe,
> Wĩth loss ŏĺ *Edĕn*, tiĺl oñe grēatĕr Man
> Rĕstoŕe ŭs, anđ rĕgain thĕ bĺissfŭl Seāt,
> Sĩng Heav̄'nĺy Muse, thăt ōn thĕ sēcret tōp
> Ŏĺ *Ōrĕb*, ōr oĺ *Sĭnăi*, dĭdst iñspire
> Tĥat Shēphĕrd, whō fĭrst taūght tĥe chōseñ Seēd,

Style and Versification

In the Beginning how the Heav'ns and Earth
Rose out of *Chaos*; Or if *Sion* Hill
Delight thee more, and *Siloa's* Brook that flow'd
Fast by the Oracle of God; I thence
Invoke thy aid to my advent'rous Song,
That with no middle flight intends to soar
Above th' *Aonian* Mount, while it pursues
Things unattempted yet in Prose or Rhyme.
(1.1–16)

XI

Sources: Sacred Founts

The biblical text is so central to the context of the poem that I shall quote it in full. These lines had probably been the most familiar text in the Western world for well over fifteen hundred years when Milton wrote. He could rely upon his audience to know it well. Familiarity with these lines is indispensable for an understanding of *Paradise Lost*. I quote from the King James Version (1611), with which Milton was familiar.

Chapter 1

In the beginning God created the heaven and the earth.
2 And the earth was without form, and void: and darkness was upon the face of the deep. And the Spirit of God moved upon the face of the waters.
3 And God said, Let there be light: and there was light.
4 And God saw the light, that it was good: and God divided the light from the darkness.
5 And God called the light Day, and the darkness he called Night. And the evening and the morning were the first day.
6 And God said, Let there be a firmament in the midst of the waters, and let it divide the waters from the waters.

7 And God made the firmament, and divided the waters which were under the firmament from the waters which were above the firmament: and it was so.

8 And God called the firmament Heaven. And the evening and the morning were the second day.

9 And God said, Let the waters under the heaven be gathered together unto one place, and let the dry land appear: and it was so.

10 And God called the dry land Earth; and the gathering together of the waters called he Seas: and God saw that it was good.

11 And God said, Let the earth bring forth grass, the herb yielding seed, and the fruit tree yielding fruit after his kind, whose seed is in itself upon the earth: and it was so.

12 And the earth brought forth grass, and herb yielding seed after his kind, and the tree yielding fruit, whose seed was in itself, after his kind: and God saw that it was good.

13 And the evening and the morning were the third day.

14 And God said, Let there be lights in the firmament of the heaven to divide the day from the night; and let them be for signs, and for seasons, and for days and years:

15 And let them be for lights in the firmament of the heaven to give light upon the earth: and it was so.

16 And God made two great lights: the greater light to rule the day, and the lesser light to rule the night: he made the stars also.

17 And God set them in the firmament of the heaven to give light upon the earth.

18 And to rule over the day and over the night, and to divide the light from the darkness: and God saw that it was good.

19 And the evening and the morning were the fourth day.

20 And God said, Let the waters bring forth abundantly the moving creature that hath life, and fowl that may fly above the earth in the open firmament of heaven.

21 And God created great whales, and every living creature that moveth, which the waters brought forth abundantly, after their kind, and every winged fowl after his kind: and God saw that it was good.

22 And God blessed them, saying, Be fruitful, and multiply, and fill the waters in the seas, and let fowl multiply in the earth.

23 And the evening and the morning were the fifth day.

24 And God said, Let the earth bring forth the living creature after his kind, cattle and creeping thing, and beast of the earth after his kind: and it was so.

25 And God made the beast of the earth after his kind, and cattle after their kind, and every thing that creepeth upon the earth after his kind: and God saw that it was good.

26 And God said, Let us make man in our image, after our likeness: and let them have dominion over the fish from the sea, and over the fowl of the air, and over the cattle, and over all the earth, and over every creeping thing that creepeth upon the earth.

27 So God created man in his own image, in the image of God created he him: male and female created he them.

28 And God blessed them, and God said unto them, Be Fruitful, and multiply, and replenish the earth, and subdue it: and have dominion over the fish of the sea, and over the fowl of the air, and over every living thing that moveth upon the earth.

29 And God said, Behold, I have given you every herb bearing seed, which is upon the face of all the earth, and every tree, in the which is the fruit of a tree yielding seed; to you it shall be for meat.

30 And to every beast of the earth, and to every fowl of the air, and to every thing that creepeth upon the earth, wherein there is life, I have given every green herb for meat: and it was so.

31 And God saw every thing that he had made, and, behold, it was very good. And the evening and the morning were the sixth day.

Chapter 2

Thus the heavens and the earth were finished, and all the host of them.

2 And on the seventh day God ended his work which he had made; and he rested on the seventh day from all his work which he had made.

3 And God blessed the seventh day, and sanctified it: because that in it he had rested from all his work which God created and made.

4 These are the generations of the heavens and of the earth when they were created, in the day that the Lord God made the earth and the heavens.

5 And every plant of the field before it was in the earth, and every herb of the field before it grew: for the Lord God had not caused it to rain upon the earth, and there was not a man to till the ground.

6 But there went up a mist from the earth, and watered the whole face of the ground.

7 And the Lord God formed man of the dust of the ground, and

breathed into his nostrils the breath of life; and man became a living
soul.

8 And the Lord God planted a garden eastward in Eden; and there
he put the man whom he had formed.

9 And out of the ground made the Lord God to grow every tree
that is pleasant to the sight, and good for food; the tree of life also
in the midst of the garden, and the tree of knowledge of good and
evil.

10 And a river went out of Eden to water the garden; and from
thence it was parted and became into four heads.

11 The name of the first is Pison: that is it which compasseth the
whole land of Havilah, where there is gold;

12 And the gold of that land is good: there is bdellium and the onyx
stone.

13 And the name of the second river is Gihon: the same it is that
compasseth the whole land of Ethiopia.

14 And the name of the third river is Hiddekel: that is it which
goeth toward the east of Assyria. And the fourth river is Euphrates.

15 And the Lord God took the man, and put him into the garden
of Eden to dress it and to keep it.

16 And the Lord God commanded the man, saying, Of every tree
of the garden thou mayest freely eat:

17 But of the tree of the knowledge of good and evil, thou shalt not
eat of it: for in the day that thou eatest thereof thou shalt surely
die.

18 And the Lord God said, It is not good that the man should be
alone; I will make him an help meet for him.

19 And out of the ground the Lord formed every beast of the field,
and every fowl of the air; and brought them unto Adam to see what
he would call them: and whatsoever Adam called every living creature, that was the name thereof.

20 And Adam gave names to all cattle, and to the fowl of the air,
and to every beast of the field; but for Adam there was not found
an help meet for him.

21 And the Lord God caused a deep sleep to fall upon Adam, and
he slept: and he took one of his ribs, and closed up the flesh instead
thereof;

22 And the rib, which the Lord God had taken from man, made he
a woman and brought her unto the man.

23 And Adam said, This is now bone of my bones, and flesh of my

flesh: she shall be called Woman, because she was taken out of Man.

24 Therefore shall a man leave his father and mother, and shall cleave unto his wife: and they shall be one flesh.

25 And they were both naked the man and his wife, and were not ashamed.

Chapter 3

Now the serpent was more subtil than any beast of the field which the Lord God had made. And he said unto the woman, Yea, hath God said, Ye shall not eat of every tree of the garden?

2 And the woman said unto the serpent, We may eat of the fruit of the trees of the garden:

3 But of the fruit of the tree which is in the midst of the garden, God hath said, Ye shall not eat of it, neither shall ye touch it, lest ye die.

4 And the serpent said unto the woman, Ye shall not surely die:

5 For God doth know that in the day ye eat thereof, then your eyes shall be opened, and ye shall be as gods, knowing good and evil.

6 And when the woman saw that the tree was good for food, and that it was pleasant to the eyes, and a tree to be desired to make one wise, she took of the fruit thereof, and did eat, and gave also unto her husband with her: and he did eat.

7 And the eyes of them both were opened, and they knew that they were naked; and they sewed fig leaves together and made themselves aprons.

8 And they heard the voice of the Lord God walking in the garden in the cool of the day: and Adam and his wife hid themselves from the presence of the Lord God among the trees of the garden.

9 And the Lord God called unto Adam, and said unto him, Where art thou?

10 And he said, I heard thy voice in the garden, and I was afraid, because I was naked; and I hid myself.

11 And he said, Who told thee that thou wast naked? Hast thou eaten of the tree, whereof I commanded thee that thou shouldest not eat?

12 And the man said, The woman whom thou gavest to be with me, she gave me of the tree, and I did eat.

13 And the Lord God said unto the woman, What is this that thou

hast done? And the woman said, The serpent beguiled me and I did eat.

14 And the Lord God said unto the serpent, Because thou hast done this, thou art cursed above all cattle, and above every beast of the field; upon thy belly shalt thou go, and dust shalt thou eat all the days of thy life:

15 And I will put enmity between thee and the woman, and between thy seed and her seed; it shall bruise thy head, and thou shalt bruise his heel.

16 Unto the woman he said, I will greatly multiply thy sorrow and thy conception; in sorrow thou shalt bring forth children; and thy desire shall be to thy husband, and he shall rule over thee.

17 And unto Adam he said, Because thou hast hearkened unto the voice of thy wife, and hast eaten of the tree, of which I commanded thee, saying, Thou shalt not eat of it: cursed is the ground for thy sake; in sorrow shalt thou eat of it all the days of thy life;

18 Thorns also and thistles shall it bring forth to thee; and thou shalt eat the herb of the field;

19 In the sweat of thy face shalt thou eat bread, till thou return unto the ground; for out of it wast thou taken: for dust thou art, and unto dust shalt thou return.

20 And Adam called his wife's name Eve; because she was the mother of all living.

21 Unto Adam and to his wife did the Lord God make coats of skins, and clothed them.

22 And the Lord God said, Behold, the man is become as one of us, to know good and evil: and now, lest he put forth his hand, and take also of the tree of life, and eat, and live forever:

23 Therefore the Lord God sent him forth from the garden of Eden, to till the ground from whence he was taken.

24 So he drove out the man; and he placed at the east of the garden of Eden Cherubims, and a flaming sword which turned every way, to keep the way of the tree of life.

Milton forces us to notice his sources, even if we choose to ignore the long beard of footnotes bristling with wisdom at the foot of the pages of *Paradise Lost*. His story has already been told in the Bible, yet the bard can claim that his poem will reveal: "things unattempted yet in Prose or Rhyme" (1.16). Milton acknowledges sources, even challenges us to examine those sources in order to understand how he is being original and how he is reinterpreting earlier works. In one sense his poem is a gloss on the first three chapters of Genesis quoted above, but Milton has taken the biblical story, which appears in almost anecdotal bareness, and expanded it by giving life, manners, and philosophy to the characters: the Father, the Son, the angels, the devils, Satan, Adam, Eve, and the narrator. His lines echo throughout the Bible. In order to understand Milton's allusions to Scripture we must remember that to Milton the Bible was a metaphor through which we are to understand the nature of God.

If the Bible is a metaphor, then Milton, if he is truly inspired to write the poem, can create his metaphor, *Paradise Lost,* from the spiritual truths he intuits. Often Milton's allusions function in the context of the original work and gain depth in this way. These allusions are the result of Milton's imaginative synthesis of what he read and thought. Milton was a creative reader who interacted with texts. Such interactions appear in his epic and range in significance from questionable rhythmic echoes to extensive allusions and discussions. A simple example would be Eve's words to Adam after the Fall: "both have sinn'd, but thou / Against God only, I against God and thee" (10.930–31). Milton's religious audience might well have remembered Psalm 51: "Against thee, thee only, have I sinned, and done this evil in thy sight: that thou mightest be justified when thou speakest, and be clear when thou judgest" (4). This psalm, attributed to King David after he had "gone in" to Bathsheba, is a classic lament and prayer for forgiveness. If we parallel this text to the passage from Milton, we feel not only that Eve's sin is earlier and her utterance the prototype of David's, but that Eve's is the greater—epic needs to be grand—because she sinned against Adam by giving him the fruit and encouraging him to eat and by explicitly disobeying God's commandment. If we look further at the context, we would read that David partly exonerates himself by saying that he was "shapen in iniquity; and in sin did my mother conceive me" (5). But Eve has no such extenuations from birth or conception. Moreover Eve's trespass is the origin in a sense of David's because he was born fallen. It is difficult to limit such reverberations (and no doubt they can descend into mere wool-gathering) but there can be no doubt that such was Milton's method.

What has been said of biblical sources may be said of all the sources of *Paradise Lost,* particularly of the next major influence—the classical epics of Homer and Virgil. Milton deliberately fused Christianity and classical antiquity, as many Renaissance writers did. Milton was very clear that Virgil and Homer were models for an epic, thereby suggesting that one learned to compose epic poetry by imitation and emulation of preferred sources. In his *Reason of Church Government,* he writes: "Time servs not now, and perhaps I might seem too profuse to give any certain account of what the mind at home in the spacious circuits of her musing hath liberty to propose to her self, though of highest hope, and hardest attempting, whether that Epick form whereof the two poems of *Homer,* and those other two of *Virgil* and *Tasso* are a diffuse . . . model: or whether the rules of *Aristotle* herein are strictly to be kept, or nature to be follow'd, which in them that know art, and use judgement is no transgression, but an inriching of art." (Prose, 1:812–13)

In *Of Education,* Milton adds others who wrote of "that sublime art which in *Aristotles poetics,* in *Horace,* and the *Italian* commentaries of *Castelvetro, Tasso, Mazzoni,* and others, teaches what the laws are of a true *Epic* poem, what of a *Dramatic,* what of a *Lyric,* what decorum [level of diction] is, which is the grand master peece to observe" (Prose, 2:404–5). Milton, in the spirit of the Renaissance, recommends the classical and Italian critics and the classical poets. The only Italian poet is Tasso, whose patron, Giovanni Battista Manso, Milton had met on his Italian journey. Tasso had written a Christian epic based on classical models. By the time Milton composed *Paradise Lost* some twenty years later, he brought in the classical epic poems in direct emulation. First he prophesies in the first invocation to the muse, the Holy Spirit, that his poem will "soar / Above th' *Aonian* Mount" (1.14–15), that is above the classical poets, who were inspired by the springs of Mount Helicon in Greece. By the climactic book 9, the narrator proclaims his story greater than Homer's *Iliad,* whose hero is Achilles; greater than Homer's *Odyssey,* whose hero was tormented by Neptune's ire; and greater than Virgil's *Aeneid*, whose hero, Cytherea's son, was tormented by Juno and fought Turnus for Lavinia. To relate the Fall is a:

> Sad Task, yet argument
> Not less but more Heroic than the wrath
> Of stern *Achilles* on his Foe pursu'd
> Thrice Fugitive about Troy Wall; or rage
> Of *Turnus* for *Lavinia* disespous'd,
> Or *Neptune's* ire or *Juno's,* that so long
> Perplex'd the *Greek* and *Cytherea's* Son.
> (9.13—19)

Milton deliberately sought common ground between the Bible and the three major epics so that one reference could touch several major (and several minor) sources. The central events of the Christian and the classical worlds had, after all, many more parallels: to name one, the apple of discord that brought about the fall of Troy was like the apple that brought about the Fall of man. Sometimes the parallels are situational. Virgil opens his epic with Aeneas and his crew foundering in the Aegean because of the wrath of the goddess Juno. Milton's opening is similar: Satan and his followers have been routed by the anger of God and are foundering on the burning lake. Both armies are searching for a new home. In order to emphasize the zeal of building Carthage and of building Pandemonium, both poets resort to similes of bees (*Aen.* 1.430–36 and PL 1.768–75). Allusions strengthen these parallels. Another "context" is Milton's echoing Virgil's description of the palace in Carthage by his description of the palace of Pandemonium right down to book and line number:

> from the arched roof
> Pendant by subtle Magic many a row
> Of Starry Lamps and blazing Cressets fed
> With *Naphtha* and *Asphaltus* yielded light
> As from a sky.
> (PL 1.726–30)

(dependent lychni laquearibus aureis
incensi et noctem flammis funalia uincunt.
(*Aen.* 1.726–27).[27]

(Burning chandeliers hang from the gold ceiling and torches conquer the night with their flames.) (my translation)

"Cressets" (torch baskets) is a literal translation of what Virgil meant
by *funalia.*

Such paralleling between the epics is constant. Milton's use of epic
conventions rather than the biblical methods he employed in *Paradise
Regained* keeps the reader alert for such parallels. Sometimes delib-
erate allusion appears. If, when Satan begins his journey toward earth,
we did not think of Odysseus's journey in the *Odyssey* to his home-
land, the narrator forces the parallel on our attention with a note of
epic emulation: Satan is "harder beset / And more endanger'd" than
"when *Ulysses* on the Larboard shunn'd / *Charybdis,* and by th' other
whirlpool steer'd" (2.1016–17; 1019–20).

Allusions to the classical epics of Homer and Virgil appear in hell,
in Eden, and in heaven. In order to warn Satan of his inevitable loss
if he fights with the angelic guards of Eden, the Father holds up the
scales of Zeus (4.996–1004; cf. *Il.* 8.69–74 and 22.209–13). The
earth in *Paradise Lost* hangs by a gold chain (2.1005; 1051–53), just
as Zeus claims he can haul up the earth to Olympus by a gold chain
(*Il* 8.19–27). If in the *Iliad* (1.590–94) Homer records that Zeus (Jove)
threw Mulciber (Hephaistos) down from heaven to Lemnos, Milton
invokes the parallel for the fall of the architect of hell and juxtaposes
Zeus and the Father:

> In ancient *Greece*; and in *Ausonian* Land
> Men call'd him *Mulciber*; and how he fell
> From Heav'n, they fabl'd, thrown by angry *Jove*
> Sheer o'er the Crystal Battlements: from Morn
> To Noon he fell, from Noon to dewy Eve,
> A Summer's day; and with the setting Sun
> Dropt from the Zenith like a falling Star,

On *Lemnos,* th' *Aegean* Isle.
(1.739–46)

In the parallels to the Bible and to the classical epics, Milton sometimes invokes the context of the original source, thus making his reference a commentary on it. For instance, he appends to the last quotation "thus they relate, / Erring" (1.746–47). This appendix could be placed after many of Milton's allusions: sometimes he corrects classical wisdom with Christian truth; sometimes he fleshes out revelation. One way or another, Milton invokes the whole literary tradition before him, making his poem encyclopedic, without making it derivative, by revising his sources. One can appreciate the poem without this wealth of allusion, but the poem is thus not felt in its true depth. *Paradise Lost* reaches out into too many directions for any one mind to comprehend (although tracking its signs has provided many academic livelihoods): to Shakespeare, Dante, Ovid, Tasso (though less so than Milton's earlier reference to that poet would indicate), Plato, Galileo, Italian and Dutch religious drama, to the now little read *Divine Weeks* of Du Bartas (in Joshua Sylvester's translation) and to other "Creation" literature, Hesiod, Saint Augustine, Spenser, and to whatever else you read that was written before Milton wrote. Of no other literary work can it be so truly said that the sources are part of the poem. Milton engaged in a symposium of all past authors.

XII

Genres:
The Anticipations
of Kind

Like most Renaissance poets, Milton was conscious of the "kind" or genre he was writing in; but unlike most Renaissance poets, or poets of any other time, Milton was not content to employ inherited conventions but sought to transcend them. Each genre he wrote in—lyric, pastoral, epic, short epic, biblical tragedy—reveals his mastery of the conventions and his new use of those conventions. In *Paradise Lost* he revamps the very concept of epic poetry. But in order to appreciate this originality, we must recognize traditional conventions. These conventions are simple and unmistakable; they signal to the reader the epic poet's connection to earlier epics. I will not attempt to be definitive, but I shall list some of the most significant epic conventions. I have adapted the first seven from Hanford's *A Milton Handbook*;[28] the last twelve are my own:

1. Invocations to the muse

2. Catalogs of armies

3. Councils (which together with battles make up most epic poetry)

4. Allegories

5. Athletic games

6. Descriptions of processes (e.g., building Pandemonium)

7. Descent from Heaven

8. Descent to Hell

9. Use of recapitulator to flashback events

10. Prophecy of future history

11. Flyting (taunting) of warriors as prelude to battle

12. Dreams (as prophecy, warning, delusion, etc.)

13. Journeys

14. Opening in medias res (in the midst of the action)

15. Emphasis upon the past as being more heroic than the present

16. A world of pastoral peace shattered by war

17. Use of extended similes

18. Long speeches in formal language

19. Incorporation of other genres, especially tragedy.

Milton not only incorporates other genres but shows the proto-type, the first appearance historically, of tragedy, pastoral, georgic (farm poetry), epithalamia (marriage songs), hymns, arguments, dialogues, treatises, creation epics, prophecy, love lyric, sermon, and more than I can recognize. Milton's epic represents a kind of literary catalog, also the "story of all things," as Samuel Barrow's introductory Latin poem on *Paradise Lost* points out (3).

XIII

Composition and Text: Premeditated and Unpremeditated

We cannot determine when Milton started to contemplate writing *Paradise Lost,* but neither can we determine when he did not contemplate writing it: he seemed born to the work, from his early dedication to learning and poetry, his beginning with pastorals like an epic poet, and his distinction between the serious poet and the trivial, as in Elegy VI, written when he was twenty-one. When he was twenty-nine (1637), he promised his father that his place as a poet would be: "with the ivy and laurel of a victor. I shall no longer mingle unknown with the dull rabble and my walk shall be far from the sight of profane eyes" (*Ad Patrem,* 102–4; translation of Merritt Y. Hughes). Such confidence, though not necessarily appealing in our more democratic age, was not without foundation.

The following year, he writes in Latin verses to Tasso's patron, Manso: "O, if my lot might but bestow such a friend upon me, a friend who understands how to honor the devotees of Phoebus—if ever I shall summon back our native kings into our songs, and Arthur, waging his wars beneath the earth, or if ever I shall proclaim the magnanimous heroes of the table which their mutual fidelity made invincible, and (if only the spirit be with me) shall shatter the Saxon phalanxes under the British Mars!" (78–84; translation of Merritt Y. Hughes).

Composition and Text

In 1640, Milton entered into the Trinity manuscript, now at Trinity College, Cambridge, no less than thirty-three such subjects for projected British heroic poems. Spenser was undoubtedly an influence on Milton at the time, since his Arthuriad, *The Faerie Queene,* was still thought of as the major English epic.

When he wrote *Reason of Church Government* (1642), we find Milton still contemplating British subject matter:

> That what the greatest and choycest wits of *Athens, Rome,* or modern Italy, and those Hebrews of old did for their country, I in my proportion with this over and above of being a Christian, might doe for mine: not caring to be once nam'd abroad, though perhaps I could attaine to that, but content with these British Ilands as my world, whose fortune hath hitherto bin, that if the Athenians, as some say, made their small deeds great and renowned by their eloquent writers, *England* hath had her noble atchievments made small by the unskilfull handling of monks and mechanicks [illiterates]. (Prose, 1:812)

But besides the entries for British epics and also for religious poems in the Trinity Manuscript, we find four drafts of a biblical tragedy. Two are mere lists of characters, which have been crossed out, but two others are outlined and named "Paradise Lost" and "Adam Unparadised." The latter contains many elements, roughly sketched, later incorporated into *Paradise Lost*:

> Adam unparadiz'd
> ~~Adams Banishment~~

> The angel Gabriel, either descending or entering, shewing since this globe was created, his frequency as much on earth, as in heavn, describes Paradise, next ~~first~~ the Chorus shewing the reason of his comming to keep his watch in Paradise after Lucifers rebellion by command from god, & withall expressing his desire to see, & know more concerning this excellent new creature man. the angel Gabriel as by his name signifying a prince of power tracing paradise with a more free office ~~comes~~ passes by the station of the chorus & desired by them relates what he knew of man as the creation of Eve with

thire love, & marriage. after this Lucifer appears after his over-
throw, bemoans himself, seeks revenge on man the Chorus prepare
resistance at his first approach as last after discourse of enmity on
either side he departs wherat the chorus sings of the battell, & vic-
torie in heav'n against him & his accomplices, as before after the
first act was sung a hymn of the creation. heer again may appear
Lucifer relating, & insulting in what he had don to the destruction
of man. man next & Eve having by this time bin seduc'd by the
serpent appeares confusedly cover'd with leaves conscience in a
shape accuses him, Justice cites him to the place whither Jehova
call'd for him in the mean while the chorus entertains the stage, &
is informed by some angel the manner of his fall heer the chorus
bewailes Adams fall. Adam then & Eve returne accuse one another
but especially Adam layes the blame to his wife, is stubborn in his
offence Justice appeares reason with him convinces him the chorus
admonisheth Adam, & bids him beware by Lucifers example of
impenitence the Angel is sent to banish them out of paradise but
before causes to passe before his eyes in shapes a mask of all the
evills of this life & world he is humbl'd relents, dispaires. at last
appears Mercy comforts him & ~~brings in faith hope, & charity~~
promises the Messiah, then calls in faith, hope, and charity, in-
structs him he repents gives god the glory, submitts to his pen-
alty the chorus briefly concludes. compare this with the former
draught.[29]

We should note particularly the central role of Satan and the vision at
the end. In this form, *Paradise Lost* is a dramatic structure, something
Milton does not abandon entirely when he converts to epic.

Edward Phillips, Milton's nephew, tells us that:

But the Heighth of his Noble Fancy and Invention began now [John
Aubrey claims 1658] to be seriously and mainly imployed in a Subject worthy of such a Muse, *viz*. A Heroick Poem, Entituled, *Paradise Lost*; the Noblest in the general Esteem of Learned and
Judicious Persons, of any yet written by any either Ancient or Modern: this Subject was first designed a Tragedy, and in the Fourth
Book of the Poem there are Ten Verses, which several Years before
the Poem was begun [Aubrey says 15 or 16; c. 1642], were shewn
to me, and some others, as designed for the very beginning of the
said Tragedy. The Verses are these;

O Thou that with surpassing Glory Crown'd!
Look'st from thy sole Dominion like the God
Of this New World; at whose sight all the Stars
Hide their diminish'd Heads; to thee I call,
But with no friendly Voice; and add thy Name,
O Sun! to tell thee how I hate thy Beams
That bring to my remembrance, from what State
I fell; how Glorious once above thy Sphere;
Till Pride and worse Ambition threw me down,
Warring in Heaven, against Heaven's Glorious King.
[Cf. 4.32–41] [30]

We shall perhaps never know why Milton gave up his Arthuriad in favor of a biblical epic, but the most reasonable explanation is that his growing dissatisfaction with the English Revolution and with England's being the chief seat of human liberty, combined with a desire to write the most universal subject of his time, perhaps of all time, the myth of Fall and redemption, caused a reluctance to write the epic of Arthur.

Of Milton's habit of composition, we have an account by another nephew, John Phillips: "Hee rendrd his Studies and various Works more easy & pleasant by allotting them thir several portions of the day. Of these the time friendly to the muses fell to his Poetry; And hee waking early (as is the use of temperate men) had commonly a good Stock of Verses ready against his Amanuensis came; which if it happend to bee later than ordinary, hee would complain, Saying *hee wanted to bee milkd.*"[31]

In 1665, Milton showed the manuscript of *Paradise Lost* to his young friend Thomas Ellwood. Milton signed the contract on 27 April 1667. In that year, *Paradise Lost* appeared in ten books. In the second edition of 1674, books 7 and 10 were split and became 7 and 8 and 11 and 12, respectively. At the request of the publisher, Samuel Simmons, Milton added the arguments that mercifully give plot summaries of the action at the beginning of each book. He also added his attack on rhyme. The blind poet probably had little control over printing, since printers went their own way then. He made ten pounds on the book, five per cent of his highest annual salary as a civil servant.

Notes

1. William Riley Parker, *Milton: A Biography* (Oxford: Clarendon Press, 1968), 1:571.

2. W. H. Auden, *The Dyer's Hand* (London: Faber and Faber, 1963), 37.

3. Lionel Trilling, *E. M. Forster* (Norfolk, Conn.: New Directions, 1943), 9.

4. A. E. Housman, *The Collected Poems of A. E. Housman* (New York: Holt, Rinehart and Winston, 1965), 88.

5. Sir Edward Marsh, *A Number of People* (New York and London: Harper, 1939), 27.

6. Ralph Hodgson, *Collected Poems* (London: Macmillan, 1961), 65.

7. John Dryden, *The Poems of John Dryden,* ed. James Kinsley (London: Clarendon Press, 1958), 2:540.

8. John Dryden, *Essays of John Dryden,* ed. W. P. Ker (Oxford: Clarendon Press, 1900), 2:165.

9. Joseph Addison, *The Spectator,* ed. Donald F. Bond (Oxford: Clarendon Press, 1956), 3:234.

10. Joseph Addison, *The Spectator,* 3:36–37.

11. Samuel Johnson, *Lives of the English Poets,* ed. George Birbeck Hill (Oxford: Clarendon Press, 1905), 1:157.

12. Ibid., 1:157.

13. Ibid., 1:194.

14. Ibid., 1:183.

15. Ibid., 1:183.

16. Ibid., 1:190.

17. William Blake, *The Complete Writings of William Blake,* ed. Geoffrey Keynes (London: Oxford University Press, 1966), 150.

18. Blake, 480.

19. William Hazlitt, *The Complete Works of William Hazlitt,* ed. P. P. Howe (London: Dent, 1930–34), 5:65.

20. Walter A. Raleigh, *Milton* (London: E. Arnold; New York: Putnam, 1900), 175.

21. E. M. W. Tillyard, *Milton,* rev. ed. (London: Chatto & Windus, 1966), 202.

22. T. S. Eliot, *On Poetry and Poets* (New York: Noonday, 1961), 156.

23. Barbara Kiefer Lewalski, *Paradise Lost and the Rhetoric of Literary Forms* (Princeton: Princeton University Press, 1985), 190–219.

24. Walter Savage Landor, "Southey and Landor," in *Milton Criticism: Selections from Four Centuries,* ed. James Thorpe (New York: Holt, Rinehart & Winston, 1950), 368.

25. James Holly Hanford and James G. Taafe, *A Milton Handbook,* 5th ed. (New York: Appleton-Century-Crofts, 1970), 244–46; Raymond Dexter Havens, *The Influence of Milton on English Poetry* (Cambridge, Mass.: Harvard University Press, 1922), 80–88.

26. George Saintsbury, *A History of English Prosody* (London: Macmillan, 1906–10), 2:271.

27. *P. Virgili Maronis Opera,* ed. R. A. B. Mynors (Oxford: Clarendon Press, 1969).

28. Hanford and Taafe, *A Milton Handbook,* 206–7.

29. *John Milton: Poems* (Menston Ilkley: Scolar Press, 1970), 38.

30. Helen Darbishire, ed., *The Early Lives of Milton* (London: Constable, 1932), 72—73.

31. Ibid., 33.

Selected Bibliography

Some Background Sources

Homer, *Iliad.*
Homer, *Odyssey.*
Aristotle, *Nicomachaean Ethics; Poetics.*
Virgil, *Aeneid.*
The Bible (King James Version. Especially *Genesis, Exodus, Job, Psalms, Isa-iah, Gospels, Revelation*).
St. Augustine, *City of God.*
Tasso, *Jerusalem Delivered.* Translated by Edward Fairfax.
Guillaume Du Bartas, *The Divine Weekes and Workes.* Translated by Joshua Sylvester.

Primary Sources

(Dates refer only to original publication.)
The Poetical Works of Mr. John Milton. Annotated by Patrick Hume. London: J. Tonson, 1695.
The Poetical Works of John Milton. Edited by H. J. Todd. 2d Ed. 7 vols. London: J. Johnson, 1809. Variorum.
Paradise Lost. Edited by Thomas Newton. 2 vols. London: J. & R. Tonson, & S. Draper, 1749. Notes.
Paradise Lost. Edited by A. W. Verity. 2 vols. Cambridge: Cambridge University Press, 1921. Allusions.

The Works of John Milton. Edited by Frank Allen Paterson. 18 vols. New York: Columbia University Press, 1931–38. Contains useful index. Latin prose texts.

The English Poems of John Milton. London: Oxford University Press, 1942. World's Classics. Contains Charles Williams's Essay.

The Poetical Works of John Milton. Edited by Helen Darbishire. 2 vols. Oxford: Clarendon Press, 1952–55. Scholarly text.

Complete Prose Works of John Milton. Edited by Don M. Wolfe, et al. 8 Vols. New Haven: Yale University Press, 1953–82. Standard edition of prose.

John Milton: Complete Poems and Major Prose. Edited by Merritt Y. Hughes. New York: Odyssey Press, 1957. Standard edition of poetry.

The Poems of John Milton. Edited by John Carey and Alastair Fowler. London: Longmans Green, 1968. Incorporates much criticism.

John Milton: Poems. Menston Ilkley: Scolar Press, 1970. Facsimile of the Trinity Manuscript.

Secondary Sources

Adams, Robert M. *Ikon: John Milton and the Modern Critics.* Ithaca: Cornell University Press, 1955.

Addison, Joseph. *Addison: Criticisms of Paradise Lost.* Edited by Albert S. Cook. Boston: Ginn, 1892. *Spectator Papers* 267, 273, 279, 285, 291, 297, 303, 309, 315, 321, 327, 333, 339, 345, 351, 357, 363, 369. Aristotelian analysis.

Berry, Boyd M. *Puritan and Religious Writing and Paradise Lost.* Baltimore and London: Johns Hopkins University Press, 1976.

Blessington, Francis C. *Paradise Lost and the Classical Epic.* London: Routledge & Kegan Paul, 1979. Homer, Virgil, Milton.

Bowra, C. M. *From Virgil to Milton.* London: Macmillan, 1945. Virgil, Camoens, Tasso.

Bridges, Robert. *Milton's Prosody.* Oxford: Oxford University Press, 1921.

Broadbent, J. B. *Some Graver Subject: An Essay on Paradise Lost.* London: Chatto and Windus, 1960. Rhetoric; symbolism.

Burden, Dennis H. *The Logical Epic: A Study of the Argument of Paradise Lost.* London: Routledge & Kegan Paul; Cambridge, Mass.: Harvard University Press, 1967.

Bush, Douglas. *English Literature in the Earlier Seventeenth Century* 1600–1660. 2d ed. Oxford: Clarendon Press, 1962. Standard literary history of the period.

Selected Bibliography

————. *Paradise Lost in our Time.* Ithaca: Cornell University Press; London: Milford, 1945. Universality of meaning.

Cohen, Kitty. *The Throne and the Chariot: Studies in Milton's Hebraism.* The Hague: Mouton, 1975.

Cope, Jackson. *The Metaphoric Structure of Paradise Lost.* Baltimore: Johns Hopkins University Press, 1962.

Corcoran, Sister Mary Irma. *Milton's Paradise with Reference to the Hexemeral Background.* Washington: Catholic University of America Press, 1945. Creation literature.

Crosman, Robert. *Reading Paradise Lost.* Bloomington: Indiana University Press, 1980. Reader response.

Curry, Walter Clyde. *Milton's Ontology, Cosmology, and Physics.* Lexington: University of Kentucky Press, 1957.

Danielson, Dennis Richard. *Milton's Good God: A Study in Literary Theodicy.* Cambridge: Cambridge University Press, 1982.

Darbishire, Helen, ed. *The Early Lives of Milton.* London: Constable, 1932. (Aubrey, J. Phillips, à Wood, E. Phillips, Toland, Richardson.)

Davies, Stevie. *Images of Kingship in Paradise Lost.* Columbia: University of Missouri Press, 1983.

Demaray, John G. *Milton's Theatrical Epic: The Invention and Design of Paradise Lost.* Cambridge, Mass.: Harvard University Press, 1981.

Diekhoff, John S. *Milton's Paradise Lost, A Commentary on the Argument.* New York: Columbia University Press; London: Oxford University Press, 1946. Logic and rhetoric.

Duncan, Joseph E. *Milton's Earthly Paradise: A Historical Study of Eden.* Minneapolis: University of Minnesota Press, 1972.

Eliot, T. S. *On Poetry and Poets.* New York: Noonday, 1961. Contains his two earlier Milton essays.

Empson, William. *Milton's God.* Rev. ed. London: Chatto and Windus, 1965. Deliberately provocative attack on Milton and on Christianity.

Evans, John M. *Paradise Lost and the Genesis Tradition.* New York: Oxford University Press, 1968.

Ferry, Anne Davidson. *Milton's Epic Voice: The Narrator in Paradise Lost.* Cambridge, Mass.: Harvard University Press, 1963.

Fiore, Peter Amadeus. *Milton and Augustine: Patterns of Augustine Thought in Paradise Lost.* University Park: Pennsylvania State University Press, 1981.

Fish, Stanley E. *Surprised by Sin: The Reader in Paradise Lost.* London: Macmillan; New York: St. Martin's, 1967. Reader response; the guilty reader.

Fixler, Michael. *Milton and the Kingdoms of God.* Evanston: Northwestern University Press; London: Faber & Faber, 1964. Ideal poem.

Fletcher, Harris Francis. *Contributions to a Milton Bibliography, 1800–1930, Being a List of Addenda to Stevens's Reference Guide to Milton.* Urbana: University of Illinois Press, 1931.

Freeman, James A. *Milton and the Martial Muse.* Princeton: Princeton University Press, 1980.

Frye, Roland M. *Milton's Imagery and the Visual Arts.* Princeton: Princeton University Press, 1978. Renaissance art.

Fuller, Elizabeth Ely. *Milton's Kinesthetic Vision in Paradise Lost.* Lewisburg: Bucknell University Press, 1983.

Gardner, Helen. *A Reading of Paradise Lost.* Oxford: Clarendon Press, 1965. Sources in painting, drama.

Gilbert, Allan H. *On the Composition of Paradise Lost.* Chapel Hill: University of North Carolina Press, 1947. Extensive theory.

Grose, Christopher. *Milton's Epic Process: Paradise Lost and its Miltonic Background.* New Haven: Yale University Press, 1973. Rhetoric.

Hamlet, Desmond M. *Justice and Damnation in Paradise Lost.* Lewisburg: Bucknell University Press, 1976.

Hanford, James Holly and Taafe, James G. *A Milton Handbook.* 5th ed. New York: Appleton-Century-Crofts, 1970.

Harding, Davis P. *The Club of Hercules: Studies in the Classical Background of Paradise Lost.* Urbana: University of Illinois Press, 1962.

————. *Milton and the Renaissance Ovid.* Urbana: University of Illinois Press, 1946.

Havens, Raymond Dexter. *The Influence of Milton on English Poetry.* Cambridge, Mass.: Harvard University Press, 1922.

Hill, Christopher. *Milton and the English Revolution.* London: Faber, 1977. Politics and literature.

Hollander, John. *The Figure of Echo: A Mode of Allusion in Milton and After.* Berkeley: University of California Press, 1981.

Huckabay, Calvin. *John Milton: An Annotated Bibliography: 1929–1968.* Rev. ed. Pittsburgh: Duquesne University Press, 1969. Most useful modern bibliography.

Hunter, G. K. *Paradise Lost.* London: Allen & Unwin, 1980. Selected introductory topics.

Ingram, William, and Swaim, Kathleen. *A Concordance to Milton's English Poetry.* New York: Oxford University Press, 1972. Standard concordance.

Kelley, Maurice W. *This Great Argument: A Study of Milton's De doctrina as a Gloss Upon Paradise Lost.* Princeton: Princeton University Press; Oxford: Oxford University Press, 1941.

Selected Bibliography

Kerrigan, William. *The Prophetic Milton*. Charlottesville: University of Virginia Press, 1974. Narrator-poet-prophet.

————. *The Sacred Complex: On the Psychogenesis of Paradise Lost*. Cambridge and London: Harvard University Press, 1983.

Kirconnell, Watson. *The Celestial Cycle: The Theme of Paradise Lost in World Literature*. Toronto: University of Toronto Press, 1952. Texts in translation.

Knott, John R., Jr. *Milton's Pastoral Vision: An Approach to Paradise Lost*. Chicago and London: University of Chicago Press, 1971.

Langdon, Ida. *Milton's Theory of Poetry and Fine Art*. New Haven: Yale University Press, 1924. Excerpts.

Le Comte, Edward. *A Milton Dictionary*. New York: Philosophical Library, 1961. Useful short dictionary.

————. *Milton and Sex*. New York: Columbia University Press, 1978.

Lewalski, Barbara Kiefer. *Paradise Lost and the Rhetoric of Literary Forms*. Princeton: Princeton University Press, 1985. All genres and sub-genres in the poem.

Lewis, C. S. *A Preface to Paradise Lost*. London: Oxford University Press, 1942. Influential clarification of issues.

Lieb, Michael. *The Dialectics of Creation: Patterns of Birth and Regeneration in Paradise Lost*. Amherst: University of Massachusetts Press, 1971.

————. *Poetics of the Holy: A Reading of Paradise Lost*. Chapel Hill: University of North Carolina Press, 1981.

MacCaffrey, Isabel Gamble. *Paradise Lost as "Myth."* Cambridge, Mass.: Harvard University Press, 1959. Archetypes.

McColley, Diane Kelsey. *Milton's Eve*. Urbana: University of Illinois Press, 1983.

McColley, Grant. *Paradise Lost: An Account of its Growth and Major Origins*. Chicago: Packard, 1940.

Madsen, William G. *From Shadowy Types to Truth: Studies in Milton's Symbolism*. New Haven: Yale University Press, 1968. Typology.

Martindale, Charles. *John Milton and the Transformation of Ancient Epic*. Totowa, N.J.: Barnes & Noble, 1986.

Martz, Louis L. *Poet of Exile: A Study of Milton's Poetry*. New Haven: Yale University Press, 1980. Reading of Milton's career.

Masson, David. *The Life of John Milton*. 7 vols. Cambridge and London: Macmillan, 1859–94. Standard history of Milton's times.

Milton Encyclopedia. General editor William B. Hunter. Lewisburg: Bucknell University Press, 1978–.

Milton Quarterly. Edited by Roy C. Flannagan. Athens: Ohio University, 1967–.

Milton Studies. Edited by James D. Simmonds. Pittsburgh: University of Pittsburgh Press, 1969–. Annual.

Oras, Ants. *Milton's Editors and Commentators from Patrick Hume to Henry John Todd.* Rev. ed. New York: Haskell House, 1967.

Parker, William Riley. *Milton: A Biography.* 2 vols. Oxford: Clarendon Press, 1968. Standard biography.

Patrides, C. A. *Milton and the Christian Tradition.* Oxford: Clarendon Press, 1968.

Peter, John. *A Critique of Paradise Lost.* London: Longmans; New York: Columbia University Press, 1960. Did Milton nod?

PMLA: Publications of the Modern Language Association of America: Bibliography. Contains standard annual bibliography of Milton.

Quilligan, Maureen. *Milton's Spenser: The Politics of Reading.* Ithaca: Cornell University Press, 1983.

Rajan, B. *Paradise Lost and the Seventeenth Century Reader.* London: Chatto and Windus, 1947.

Raleigh, Sir Walter A. *Milton.* London: E. Arnold; New York: Putnam, 1900. Epic and epic style.

Revard, Stella Purce. *The War in Heaven: Paradise Lost and the Tradition of Satan's Rebellion.* Ithaca: Cornell University Press, 1980.

Ricks, Christopher. *Milton's Grand Style.* Oxford: Oxford University Press, 1963. Subtleties of Milton's style to vindicate him from the Cambridge attack.

Riggs, William G. *The Christian Poet in Paradise Lost.* Berkeley and London: University of California Press, 1972.

Ryken, Leland. *The Apocalyptic Vision in Paradise Lost.* Ithaca and London: Cornell University Press, 1970.

Saurat, Denis. *Milton: Man and Thinker.* 2nd. ed. London: Dent, 1944.

Samuel, Irene. *Dante and Milton.* Ithaca: Cornell University Press, 1947.

Shawcrosse, John T. *With Mortal Voice: The Creation of Paradise Lost.* Lexington: University of Kentucky Press, 1982.

Shoaf, R. A. *Milton, Poet of Duality.* New Haven: Yale University Press, 1985.

Shumacher, Wayne. *Unpremeditated Verse: Feeling and Perception in Paradise Lost.* Princeton: Princeton University Press, 1967.

Sims, James H. *The Bible in Milton's Epics.* Gainesville: University of Florida Press, 1962.

Smith, Logan Pearsall. *Milton and His Modern Critics.* London: Oxford University Press, 1940.

Spaeth, Sigmund G. *Milton's Knowledge of Music.* Princeton: Princeton University Library, 1913.

Selected Bibliography

Sprott, S. Ernest. *Milton's Art of Prosody*. Oxford: Blackwell, 1953.

Steadman, John M. *Epic and Tragic Structure in Paradise Lost*. Chicago: University of Chicago Press, 1976.

————. *Milton and the Renaissance Hero*. Oxford: Clarendon Press, 1976.

————. *Milton's Biblical and Classical Imagery*. Pittsburgh: Duquesne University Press, 1984.

————. *Milton's Epic Characters: Image and Idol*. Chapel Hill: University of North Carolina Press, 1968.

Stein, Arnold. *Answerable Style: Essays on Paradise Lost*. Minneapolis: University of Minnesota Press, 1953.

————. *The Art of Presence: The Poet and Paradise Lost*. Berkeley and London: University of California Press, 1977.

Stevens, David Harrison. *A Reference Guide to Milton from 1800 to the Present Day*. Chicago: University of Chicago Press, 1930.

Summers, Joseph H. *The Muse's Method: An Introduction to Paradise Lost*. Cambridge, Mass.: Harvard University Press; London: Chatto & Windus, 1962.

Svendsen, Kester. *Milton and Science*. Cambridge, Mass.: Harvard University Press, 1956.

Tayler, Edward W. *Milton's Poetry: Its Development in Time*. Pittsburgh: Duquesne University Press, 1978.

Thorpe, James, ed. *Milton Criticism: Selections from Four Centuries*. New York: Holt, Rinehart and Winston, 1950. Contains basic passages from Dryden, Johnson, Blake, Shelley, Emerson, Arnold, and others.

Tillyard, E. M. W. *Milton*. Rev. ed. London: Chatto and Windus, 1966. Conscious and unconscious meanings.

A Variorum Commentary on the Poems of John Milton. General editor Merritt Y. Hughes. New York: Columbia University Press, 1970–.

Waldock, A. J. A. *Paradise Lost and its Critics*. Cambridge: Cambridge University Press, 1947. Part of "Cambridge attack."

Webber, Joan Malory. *Milton and his Epic Tradition*. Seattle and London: University of Washington Press, 1979. Tradition in Jungian metaphor.

Werblowsky, R. J. Zwi. *Lucifer and Prometheus: A Study of Milton's Satan*. London: Routledge & Kegan Paul, 1952.

West, Robert H. *Milton and the Angels*. Athens: University of Georgia Press, 1955.

Whaler, James. *Counterpoint and Symbol. An Inquiry into the Rhythm of Milton's Epic Simile*. Copenhagen: Rosenkilde & Bagger, 1956.

Wheeler, Thomas. *Paradise Lost and the Modern Reader*. Athens: University of Georgia Press, 1974.

Wilson, A. N. *The Life of John Milton*. Oxford: Oxford University Press, 1983. Good read.

Woodhull, Mariana. *The Epic of Paradise Lost*. New York: Putnam, 1907. Epic, tragedy, sources.

Wright, B. A. *Milton's Paradise Lost*. London: Methuen; New York: Barnes and Noble, 1962. Defends Milton.

Index

Index

About the Author

Francis C. Blessington was born in Boston, Massachusetts. He graduated from Boston College, Northeastern University, and Brown, from which he holds an A.M. in classics and a Ph.D. in English. A widely published critic and poet, he has written *Paradise Lost and the Classical Epic* (London: Routledge & Kegan Paul, 1979), *The Motive for Metaphor: Essays on Modern Poetry in Honor of Samuel French Morse,* edited with Guy Rotella (Boston: Northeastern University Press, 1983), and *Lantskip* (poems) (Dublin, N.H.: William L. Bauhan, 1987). He is a professor of English at Northeastern University.